An OPUS book

Why Punish?

Why Punish?

NIGEL WALKER

Oxford   New York

OXFORD UNIVERSITY PRESS

1991

Oxford University Press, Walton Street, Oxford OX2 6DP

Oxford New York Toronto
Delhi Bombay Calcutta Madras Karachi
Petaling Jaya Singapore Hong Kong Tokyo
Nairobi Dar es Salaam Cape Town
Melbourne Auckland
and associated companies in
Berlin Ibadan

Oxford is a trade mark of Oxford University Press

British Library Cataloguing in Publication Data
Walker, Nigel 1917–
Why punish?—(OPUS)
1. Offenders. Punishment
I. Title II. Series
364.601
ISBN 0–19–219240–X
ISBN 0–19–289219–3 pbk

Library of Congress Cataloging in Publication Data
Walker, Nigel.
Why punish? / Nigel Walker.
p. cm.
Includes bibliographical references and index.
1. Punishment—Philosophy. I. Title.
HV8675.W33 1991 364.6–dc20 90–25919
ISBN 0–19–219240–X
ISBN 0–19–289219–3 pbk

Typeset by Best-set Typesetter Ltd
Printed in Great Britain by
Biddles Ltd, Guildford and King's Lynn

To my wife

Preface

THE title of this book is a tribute to Herbert Hart, who used it for his series of lectures at Oxford in 1959. I happened to be there on sabbatical leave from the Scottish Office, where I had been concerned with criminal justice and, in particular, with sentences of death and imprisonment. Later, after appointment to a readership at Oxford, I was invited to join Herbert Hart and Rupert Cross in seminars on punishment and responsibility. I hope that this book shows how much I learned from them, even if they would not endorse all I have to say now, a quarter of a century later.

For during the sixties and seventies I was also conducting weekly seminars of a different sort, in Oxford and Bedford prisons, with mixed groups of prisoners and students. The object was neither research nor reform, but the interchange of views on sentencing between people to whom the subject was of professional interest. The surroundings were rather different from All Souls', but the behaviour of the participants was at least as well mannered. Although prison staff were seldom present—and then only by special invitation—the whole enterprise would have been impossible without their co-operation, and I should like to record my particular thanks to two prison governors, John Brophy and Dermott Grubb, for persuading their officers that the seminars were a good thing for the prisoners. They were certainly good for the academic participants, since they made us aware of the reactions and reasoning of men who were experiencing official punishment, some of them for the first time but some of them for the nth time. Their insights are reflected here and there in this book.

Discussions of a third kind, with sentencers on committees and at conferences, made me aware that while they are expected to know their law they are not encouraged to agonize about objectives. I have known magistrates who confused retribution with deterrence, and judges of appeal who confused it with denunciation. Reports of committees hurry past the fundamental issues because the draftsmen want to avoid dissension. Writers of textbooks on criminal law dispose of them in a few smooth paragraphs, knowing that they are skating on thin ice, with deep waters underneath.

The deep waters are where the moral philosophers lurk, preying like sharks on each other and on practitioners who are careless enough to put their feet through the ice. A few are amphibious, and surface to study the realities of sentencing: the Australian philosopher Chung Li Ten is a welcome example. Some, on the other hand, have little or no knowledge of recent penological research or sentencing practice. This book is an attempt to promote the amphibian way: to lure philosophers onto dry land and penologists into deep water.

To be amphibian, however, is not necessarily to be impartial. *Crime and Criminology* was criticized by one reviewer for not disclosing my own views on some issues. If that was a mistake this book does not make it. My dissatisfaction with retributivism, classical or modern, must be clear. The one issue which I have not argued to a finish is the morality of capital punishment. Campaigners who want it abolished or restored will find that here or there I discuss most of the relevant considerations, because they are not confined to the death penalty. My subject, however, is not penal reform. Nobody who has been personally involved in the proceedings which lead to an execution can, or should, forget what it means. But capital punishment is a topic which needs a whole book, and there have been many. I hope, too, that readers who dislike it will not allow this to bias them against philosophers such as Kant or Nozick when, in passing, I mention their support for it.

When an argument is relevant the reader will be offered just enough history and name-droppings to show him where it originated and how seriously it has been taken in the past. A historian's history, however, would have to be a very different sort of book. My purpose has been to consider how each idea, whatever its lineage, stands up to modern research or reasoning. Readers who want to dig deeper should find my notes and the 'Further Reading' helpful and, I hope, unbiased.

Nor can clichés be ignored, because they are a strong intellectual currency. 'Deterrents don't work' is an example, used by penal reformers who have either not studied the evidence or have imposed on it their own wishful interpretation. Rhetoric is something different. C. S. Lewis allowed it to carry him away, as we shall see in Chapter 7. Wherever I have detected it—for example in the metaphors of retributivists discussed in Chapter 9—I have tried to replace it with reasoning based on literal language. The result may not be as inspiring, but it leads to sounder conclusions.

Nigel Walker

King's College, Cambridge

Acknowledgements

I HAVE already acknowledged my debt to Herbert Hart and Rupert Cross. Some of my footnotes thank those who have helped me with specific information or references. Here I should like to record my debt to Anthony Bottoms of the Institute of Criminology at Cambridge, Joel Kupperman of the University of Connecticut, and Ian White of St John's College, Cambridge, for comments which greatly improved Part III.

My special thanks are due to Mrs Pamela Paige, who typed and retyped this book with accuracy and forbearance.

Contents

Introduction

PUNISHMENT is an institution in almost every society. Only very small and very isolated communities are at a loss about what to do with transgressors,[1] and even they recognize the punishment of children by parents. Punishment, however, has different names. When imposed by English-speaking courts it is called 'sentencing'. In the Christian Church it is 'penance'. In schools, colleges, professional organizations, clubs, trade unions, and armed forces its name is 'disciplining' or 'penalizing'. It is an institution which is exemplified in transactions involving individuals, transactions which are controlled by rules, laying down what form it is to take, who may order it, and for what.

i. Seven features of punishment

The rules of societies, organizations, and families differ, as do the rules for other social institutions such as commerce, marriage or sport. Yet underlying them there seems to be a shared conception of punishment, which has seven features:[2]

1. It involves the infliction of something which is assumed to be unwelcome to the recipient: the inconvenience of a disqualification, the hardship of incarceration, the suffering of a flogging, exclusion from the country or community, or in extreme cases death. 'Assumed to be', because the fact that a few people enjoy being flogged, or are in the fortunate position of being able to afford a fine, does not mean that these measures are not punishment. It is the assumptions of those who order something to be done that determine whether it is or is not punishment: see Feature 7.

2. The infliction is intentional and done for a reason. Accidental harm, such as an injury caused by my own bad driving, is not regarded as punishment in the strict sense. True, we sometimes say that I have been 'punished enough' by it, and Continental jurists talk of 'natural punishment' (*poena naturalis*).[3] But these are mere figures of speech, designed to

explain why we treat victims of their own misbehaviour with leniency.

3. Those who order it are regarded—by the members of the society, organization, or family—as having the right to do so. In families this right is usually regarded as confined to adults *in loco parentis*. In states and organizations the rules specify who has the right. Inflictions by others are unofficial: 'lynchings' have a special name to distinguish them from official punishment.

4. The occasion for the infliction is an action or omission which infringes a law, rule, or custom. Thoughts are no longer regarded as punishable. Mere dislike or fear of someone is not enough. This does not prevent rule-makers from expressing some of their dislikes or fears in the form of prohibitions, examples being the sumptuary[4] laws of the Romans, the exclusion of Jews from membership of clubs, or the use of vagrancy laws to inconvenience hippies. But these make most people uneasy.

5. The person punished has played a voluntary part in the infringement, or at least his punishers believe or pretend to believe that he has done so. Situations in which such a pretence might be expedient are discussed in Chapter 11. Meanwhile all that has to be noted is that some philosophers have objected that punishment must always be deserved, so that mistaken or deceitful penalizing should not be called 'punishment'. There is no harm in arguing about verbal usage, so long as the argument does not pretend to settle the question 'Should such things be done?' That cannot be answered by deciding what to call them, only by considerations of the sort set out in Chapter 11. Meanwhile, like the man in the street, we can continue to talk about 'mistaken' or 'deceitful' punishment.

6. The punisher's reason for punishing is such as to offer a justification for doing so. It must not be mere sadism, for example. Sometimes it is simply a respect for consistency: the sentencer copies his colleagues; but if so we expect at least one of his colleagues to articulate a better justification. A justification is called for because what is involved is the imposition of something unpleasant regardless of the wishes of the person on whom it is imposed (unlike dentistry, surgery, or penance, from which the sufferer would hope to benefit). Note, however, that

the punisher's justification may or may not be the justification
for the social institution called 'punishment'. In the first place,
to talk of 'the' justification for the social institution must be
speculative, if not altogether artificial. Only a naïve historian or
anthropologist would confidently assert that in a given society
the institution had been created or fostered by people whose
aim was to minimize law-breaking, or, alternatively, by people
who wanted to maximize retribution. Even today the most that
sociologists can tell us is what percentage of those who endorse
their criminal justice system subscribe to such justifications. But
when an agent of the criminal justice system is sentencing a
particular offender it is reasonable to ask him how *he* justifies
his sentence: one can talk of 'his' justification. He may of course
offer a different justification in different cases, being perhaps an
'eclectic' of one of the sorts discussed in Chapter 15; in which
case one should be more precise and talk of 'his' justification 'in
this case'. But we should avoid vague terms such as '*the*
justification for sentencing' (or 'punishment').

7. It is the belief or intention of the person who orders
something to be done, and not the belief or intention of the
person to whom it is done, that settles the question whether it is
punishment. We do not decide that a prison sentence is not
punishment because the prisoner considers it unjust, or
imagines that it is for his own protection. True, the Victorian
philosopher Thomas Hill Green thought that 'when the
specified conditions of punishment are fulfilled the person
punished himself recognises it as just, as his due or desert . . . '.[5]
Most philosophers, however, are more realistic about offenders' reactions, although—as we shall see in Chapter 9—there
are still some who build a theory around this hope.

ii. Reward

This brief introduction seems the right place in which to deal
with an old cliché: the symmetry between punishment and
reward. Rewarding people is said to be the mirror image of
punishing them. The first point to be made is that no
illuminating conclusion has ever been drawn from this observation. The second is that it is a rather superficial observation:
the differences between punishment and reward are more

interesting than the resemblances. True, rewarding is an intentional action, with a justification that can be explained, and based on the rewarder's belief that the rewardee did something meritorious and will regard the reward as a benefit. Some rewards, like most punishments, are part of a social institution, medals being an example. Some are even promised, for instance in attempts to recover missing property (although the contractual nature of such transactions distinguishes them from most kinds of reward). But that is about as far as the symmetry goes. Punishers must have a social position which authorizes them to punish, but anyone can reward. The reason for the reward need have nothing to do with the observance of laws or rules: more often rewards are for conduct 'beyond the call of duty'. People are punished, but hardly ever rewarded, against their wills. (It may be conventional to say 'I don't want (deserve) it', but a reward which genuinely distressed the recipient would hardly be a reward.)

iii. Revenge

It is more illuminating to compare punishment with revenge. As Locke pointed out, even in a 'state of nature' there would be a difference between revenging one's self on a criminal and punishing him.[6] Vengeful feelings are roused by injuries or insults to one's self or to others with whom one feels some bond. Punitive feelings are more disinterested. The occasion which calls for punishment must be a breach of some law or code of conduct: in the case of revenge it may be merely an insult or defeat in some legitimate rivalry. Yet the differences can be exaggerated. Punishments are subject to rules about consistency and appropriateness; but there are countries in which this is true of revenge. A sentencer must have a proper reason for forgoing punishment (see Chapter 14) whereas a private person may forgo revenge without having to justify himself—except, again, in cultures which 'institutionalize' revenge. Finally, although European cultures approve of punitive motives and disapprove of vengefulness, they are not always easy to distinguish. Even an official sentencer may be prompted by sympathy with a victim who is a member of his community or with whom he identifies himself in some other way. One may feel outraged when someone else does what one would have liked to do but for one's code of conduct. Is such outrage vengeful or punitive?

Most of what has been said in this Introduction—as well as a good deal of what follows—is not moral philosophy but simple sociology, of the kind that deals with the meanings ascribed to socially important words. It has been concerned with what 'punishment' means to most English-speakers who take a serious interest in the subject. It has not attempted to prescribe what punishment must be. That leads to the rhetorical trick which uses definitions to settle arguments about what may or may not be done. Feature 5 has already provided an example: penalizing people who do not 'deserve' it cannot be ruled out by a mere definition. Genuine objections will be discussed in Chapter 11, where we shall come across another example. Are sentencers 'punishing' the undeserving families of offenders whom they send to prison, if they know but do not intend the harm that this will do to those families? Merely to decide whether to call this 'punishment' does not tell us whether it is morally acceptable.

1
Justifying Sentences

MANY sentencers, too busy to worry about such matters, would justify their sentences very simply. They are what the law prescribes, what the Court of Appeal or the Magistrates' Association recommends, or what the local bench has agreed upon. A cynic might dismiss this as mere conformity; but it may be something more respectable: consistency. Inconsistencies between the sentencing of similar cases are criticized by the news media, resented by offenders, and—most important— treated by appellate courts as grounds for interference. Inconsistency is 'unfairness'.

Yet a sentencer who regards his consistency with his colleagues' practice as a complete justification is rather like a priest who performs ritual actions without asking himself why they are part of the ritual. Even a ritual has a meaning. Punishment is something more than a series of hopefully consistent decisions: as we have seen, it is a social institution. Like other social institutions it must serve—or at least appear to serve—one or more desired functions. If it did not, it would have been allowed to wither away, like outlawry and craft-guilds, or have come to be regarded as nothing more than a ritual, like the mounting of ceremonial guards.

i. The utilitarian tradition

Most people have no difficulty in identifying its utility. For them it is the reduction of the frequency with which people infringe the laws and rules which make for a contented society. It contributes to this by deterring the offender from reoffending, discouraging others from following his example, or putting him where he cannot offend any longer. It is this sort of utility which is the justification offered by utilitarians—Protagoras, Grotius, Beccaria, Bentham, Mill, Wootton.[1]

ii. The retributive tradition

The utilitarian tradition, however, has had to contend with an even older one. The Greek philosophers were rationalists, but Greek mythology was full of vengeance. The major deities of the classical Pantheon seem to have been concerned only to avenge personal insults or opposition; but there were older and darker goddesses of whom mortals were more afraid. Nemesis arranged 'natural punishments' for the wicked and the over-weening. The Erinyes—the Furies in Roman mythology—used men's minds as the instruments of justice, driving them to avenge homicides, rapes, and other crimes. Clytemnestra felt obliged to avenge Iphigenia on Agamemnon, her son felt obliged to avenge his father on her, and so on down the dynasty.

As for the religions which acknowledge Abraham as a prophet—Judaism, Christianity, and Islam—all three attach a special kind of guilt to sins: a kind that can be expiated only by sacrifice or suffering. The early Christians expressed this feeling in a formal system of penances: voluntary self-punishment. We shall see, in Chapter 9, how at least one author has used the notion of penance to justify punishment. Most penances, however, had no secular utility: they simply rendered the sinner once more eligible for salvation. Since there was an overlap between what the Church regarded as sin and the civil law regarded as crime it was natural that the law came to be seen as a way of enforcing atonement. Many judges see their sentences not only as deterrents but also as what malefactors deserve; and desert, like penance, has no secular utility.

Philosophers, too, have inherited the retributive tradition. Bentham's contemporary, Kant, was scathing about 'the serpent-windings of utilitarianism', and became the prophet of classical notions of desert. Hegel in Germany and Bradley in England were his nineteenth-century disciples.[2] The increasing appeal of utilitarian penologies in the twentieth century has been resisted by a rearguard of British and American philo-sophers, of whom Bosanquet, Armstrong, Flew, Mackie, and Nozick have been notable.[3]

iii. Legislative ambiguity

Both traditions are reflected in public opinion. Two out of
every five adults in England believe that the primary aim of
sentencers should be 'to give the offender what he deserves':
the other three endorse aims such as deterrence, public
protection, and reform.[4] It is therefore not surprising that penal
codes sit on the fence. There are exceptions. Until recently the
West German code made it clear that guilt and desert should be
the main considerations in sentencers' minds, while the post-war
Yugoslav code listed only utilitarian aims.[5] Most codes, however, are deliberately non-committal on the subject. In demo-
cracies whose members are divided about it legislators realize
that ambiguity, not honesty, is the best policy.

iv. Eclecticism

In practice Anglo-American sentencers tend to be eclectic,
reasoning sometimes as utilitarians but sometimes, when they
are outraged by a crime, as retributivists. Since a case can be
made out for either kind of reasoning, eclecticism is at least
understandable. Whether it is logically defensible is another
question, which will be considered in Chapter 15. For the
moment we are concerned with the contest between all-out
utilitarianism and all-out retributivism.

It is a tug of war in which ground is lost and won slowly,
and with different results in different cultures. The influence of
Kant has always been stronger in Germanic countries than in
Britain and North America, where Benthamism has shaped the
penal codes, allowing sentencers more freedom to depart from
the 'tariff' of penalties. Even so, the last four decades have
witnessed a progressive weakening of confidence in Bentham's
utilitarian outlook. Campaigners for the abolition of capital
punishment cast doubt on its value as a deterrent. Researchers
who compared the results of reformative measures with those of
ordinary incarceration reported findings which were disappointing. Moralists, too, produced persuasive objections, not only to
deterrents and therapies but also to preventive measures that
involved elimination or long detention.

v. Just deserts

As we shall see in the chapters that follow, the research and the reasoning did not always support the conclusions of the iconoclasts. The effect on penological thinking, however, was powerful, especially in the United States. Deterrence, rehabilitation, and precautionary detention continued to be the mainstay of official policy; but in academic circles they were decried as unattainable or unethical. The pendulum began to swing from utilitarianism back to retributivism. In 1976 an American committee, strongly influenced by the Kantian outlook of its rapporteur Andrew von Hirsch, published a report called *Doing Justice*; and 'justice' meant 'just deserts'.[6]

The report struck a responsive chord amongst legislators. In some states judges had used the freedom conferred by sentencing statutes to indulge in extreme leniency or severity,[7] sometimes as the result of undisclosed influences. Led by California, some states—and eventually the Federal system—tightened their penal codes by laying down mandatory sentences and limiting the extent to which they could be varied in aggravating or mitigating circumstances.

The report attracted less interest in Britain, where judges were more inclined to sentence according to a tariff—even if a loose and unwritten one. Only a few penologists and philosophers discussed it. Yet 'just deserts' deserved more attention, which it has begun to receive, in Scandinavia as well as in Britain.[8] It sounds at first like a revival of Kantian retributivism, but has turned out to be something different. In the first place, for Kant and his Continental followers the infliction of deserved punishment was an obvious duty. It did not matter whether it had a utilitarian value: it had a moral value. 'Just desertion', on the other hand, is the product of disillusionment with utilitarianism: a *pis aller*. What is more, as we shall see, 'just deserters' such as von Hirsch are apt to claim that the infliction of deserved punishment has utility. Finally, 'just deserters' have been forced to face problems which did not occur to Kant: problems which will be discussed in Part III.

PART I
Utilitarian Aims

THE disillusionment with utilitarianism which Chapter 1 described so briefly is the result partly of ethical misgivings which will be the subject of Part II; but chiefly of empirical attempts to measure the efficacy of sentences which are intended as deterrents, as efforts to induce or intensify law-abiding attitudes of offenders or the public, or as ways of protecting the public by making it harder for identified offenders to offend again. The chapters in Part I will explain why the research of the last few decades has been so discouraging, but will also suggest that in certain respects the discouragement has been the result of exaggerated interpretations of the evidence.

'Evidence' means different things in different contexts. When committees or commissions 'take evidence' they listen to personal views and anecdotes as well as hard facts. 'Evidence' in a court of law is what witnesses are prepared to say on oath and subject to cross-examination. For social scientists, if they are doing their job properly, evidence is harder to come by. They too may listen to individuals, but less credulously than juries. They interview as many people as their resources permit, selecting them so that they are as representative as possible of the category they are studying. They check whether what interviewees say is borne out by what they do, especially when they are offenders who claim to be deterred or reformed. They collect statistics, but also subject them to special techniques of analysis to establish the degree of confidence with which general inferences can be drawn from them. Sometimes they are able to devise experiments in which variables can be manipulated in order to see what effect this has. Occasionally changes in the law or other conditions provide them with 'quasi-experiments' of a more realistic sort.

Even the evidence of social scientists, however, may be

presented tendentiously. Penalties such as capital punishment and incarceration are emotive subjects. Most people want to see them used less often, or more often. Many books about them are by penal reformers or journalists with axes to grind, and their use of the evidence is often selective or even dishonest. Penologists are social scientists, not penal reformers, but not all of them find it easy to interpret their findings without an eye on the ways in which they may affect policy. Even when they do they cannot prevent penal reformers from imposing their own interpretations. Hence assertions such as 'The death penalty never deters' or 'Correctives never work'. 'Never' is a word that should make any penological claim suspect. Another is 'always'.

2

Deterring Others

THE deterrence of potential offenders is a traditional objective of utilitarian penologists.[1] In the mind of the man in the street it is associated with severe penalties, and in particular capital punishment or long prison sentences. Obviously the milder penalties, such as fines, are used with deterrent intentions: but it is the association with severity that has made deterrence a controversial objective, and even, in the mouths of some reformers, a dirty word. Doubts have been cast on both its attainability and its moral acceptability.

Those for whom it is morally unacceptable split into two groups. For some it is unacceptable whether it is attainable or not: we shall see why later in Chapter 6. For most it is unacceptable because they believe it to be unattainable. If, as has been claimed,[2] 'deterrents never work', to inflict suffering—or even mere inconvenience—in the name of deterrence is to do so uselessly, and therefore wrongly. So this chapter discusses the evidence for the efficacy of measures intended to deter potential offenders (the deterrence of those who have actually offended will be considered in the chapter on correction: Chapter 5).

i. Defining deterrence

Difficulties have been raised over the very definition of deterrence,[3] but are not insoluble. People are deterred from actions[4] when they *refrain* from them because they dislike what they believe to be the *possible consequences* of those actions. Each of the italicized words needs explication. Is a person deterred if he refrains there and then from an action which he performs later and perhaps elsewhere? 'Displacement' of this sort occurs when the sight of a police car makes a burglar transfer his plans to another street. From the point of view of local residents this must be welcome; but whether it should be called deterrence is doubtful. The point is hardly more than semantic: what matters is to distinguish displacement from what most people would call deterrence, and to realize that local decreases in such offences as burglary may merely be examples of the former.

As for the *consequences* which potential offenders may have in mind, they need not be penalties. Mere difficulties, such as high walls, can deter. So may dogs, or barbed wire. Such considerations can be lumped together under the heading of 'on-the-spot deterrents'.[5] More remote are consequences such as the stigma of being known as a shop-lifter, or a bad driver, amongst one's acquaintances; and of course the possibility of detection, conviction, and a penalty.

A person is not deterred if he refrains because he is not tempted, or is tempted but restrained by his code of manners or morals. It does not matter that his unresponsiveness to temptation, or his manners or morals, may be the result of deterrents applied during his formative years: he is not being deterred *now*. On the other hand, if he refrains because he knows that if he yields he will later reproach himself, it seems necessary to say that he is being deterred, just as it would be if what he feared were the reproaches of other people.

As for the *possibility* of the deterring consequences, all that matters is that the person should believe in it. His belief may be quite illusory. There may be no way in which the action he is contemplating could be brought home to him, but if he abstains because he believes it may be he is deterred. He need not believe that the consequences are at all likely: anxious people are deterred by quite remote possibilities. If the possibility is very nasty even a low degree of probability will discourage a lot of people. Many parents used to resist invitations to have their infants immunized against whooping-cough because of the very small risk that it would cause a disabling encephalitis.[6]

Deterrence may be intermittent. A young man may be too cautious to attempt a burglary on a Tuesday but do it the next day.[7] There are several well-known states of mind in which normally law-abiding men and women become temporarily undeterrable and do things whose consequences would usually deter them: fear, fury, intoxication, vengefulness, sudden sexual desire. There are even some people who can be classified as chronically undeterrable. Some mental disorders have this effect; but so too may extreme situations, such as 'death-camps' or 'skid-rows' in which the individual sees his prospects as so dismal that the consequences of law-breaking seem no worse.

The relevance of all these preliminaries is this. No sensible person has much difficulty in defining deterrence, still less in recognizing it as an everyday occurrence. Nor do sensible penologists doubt that penalties operate as deterrents. What some question is whether the nature or severity of penalties make much difference to their efficacy. They have an arguable case, of sorts. First, there are social contexts in which people can be discouraged from behaviour that infringes a rule if they are simply told that there is a rule, without mention of a penalty. New members of clubs, schools, colleges, professions, or even gangs are anxious to conform, and need no threats. Of course not everyone obeys the law as soon as it is explained to him; but fear of being detected and stigmatized as a law-breaker is enough for many. There are people, however, who do not care much about stigma. They may already have been stigmatized. In some cases what we regard as a stigma—for example a reputation for violence—has become a matter of pride. Or the incentive may be very strong. In these cases the likelihood of being penalized may turn the scale, if they are in a deterrable state of mind. What some penologists question is whether the nature or severity of the penalty adds anything to the power of the deterrent.

ii. Capital punishment and homicide

Unlikely as it may seem, capital punishment provides an impressive illustration, for the very reason that for centuries it has been regarded as a uniquely powerful deterrent. Nowadays there is an increasing number of jurisdictions in which the penal code has substituted a long and usually indefinite period of imprisonment. The United States, for example, comprises both 'abolitionist' and 'retentionist' states. Criminologists who have compared their murder-rates have found it impossible to tell from these rates which are the abolitionist states. The findings were similar in a study of a single jurisdiction in which periods of abolition alternated with periods in which the death penalty was revived. In New Zealand during the years from 1924 to 1962 it was at first in force, then abolished, then revived, then in abeyance, then abolished again. The legislators were not deliberately experimenting, but their changes of policy provided the nearest thing to an experiment that we are ever likely to see. The changes were well publicized throughout this small country, and so were the cases in which the death penalty was actually inflicted. Murder was a crime with a high detection-rate. As was to be expected with small numbers the murder-rate fluctuated.[8] But the fluctuations bore no discernible relationship to the status of the death penalty: one cannot tell from them when it was in force and when it was not.

Homicide is a crime usually committed in undeterrable states of mind. One would not expect the volume of such killings to be affected by any sort of deterrent. Some homicides, however, are premeditated, and others are committed in cold blood. Even so, the best review of the evidence from research concludes that 'it has failed to provide scientific proof that executions have a greater deterrent effect than life imprisonment. Such proof is unlikely to be forthcoming.'[9] On the whole, it seems that if a person is minded to commit a murder then either the thought of an indeterminate prison sentence will dissuade him or nothing will.[10] Long imprisonment is no deterrent for some, but a sufficient deterrent for others, *and a deterrent that is more than sufficient is not more effective.*

In more precise terms what the evidence strongly suggests is this. If a 'sufficient deterrent' is defined as one which maximizes the number of people who are deterred from some type of behaviour, then so far as homicide is concerned both capital punishment and indeterminate imprisonment seem to be sufficient deterrents. It is important to note that this statement must be confined to homicide, because all the evidence relates to that crime. It may or may not be true when capital punishment is the penalty for types of crime which are more often premeditated than homicide is. There are jurisdictions in which dealing illicitly in dangerous drugs, or engaging in illicit transactions which harm the state's economy, incur the death penalty; but we do not know whether it deters more potential offenders of those kinds than would indeterminate imprisonment.[11]

Homicide, however, is not the 'crime apart' that it is said to be. Often it is just serious personal violence that has had more drastic results than the perpetrator intended.[12] So the statistics for serious intentional injuries are relevant. A careful piece of research by an econometrist[13] who used English and Welsh data found that the rates for such violence—as well as for minor violence—varied inversely[14] with the percentage of guilty verdicts which led to imprisonment, but that their association with the average *length* of imprisonment was very weak. Clearly, if a person thinks about consequences before acting violently, what he thinks about is whether he is likely to go to prison, but not for how long.

iii. Subjective probabilities

Almost as strong, however, was the inverse association between the violence-rate and the likelihood of being identified.[15] With some kinds of crime this association is stronger than any other, the imprisonment-rate being a close second. This is important, because some penal reformers cling to the old penological cliché that the probability of conviction is the only factor in deterrence that is at all effective. They mean, of course, the *subjective* probability: the offender's own estimate of the likelihood. Statisticians can measure only the *general objective* probability.[16] Since each individual's objective probability of being convicted varies with his skill and the circumstances, and since his estimate of it further varies according to his optimism (and trust in defence lawyers), it is likely that subjective probabilities are even more closely related to the decision to commit a crime than the statistics suggest.

The same, of course, may well be true of individuals' estimates of the likelihood that a conviction will lead to imprisonment. Again statisticians can measure only the general objective probability; but econometric studies which distinguish the imprisonment-rate from the conviction-rate do not support the notion that the imprisonment-rate is a negligible factor. In some North American studies the average length of imprisonment seems also to be an important consideration, though less powerful than the imprisonment-rate.[17] In plain terms, if a person is contemplating the commission of a crime, he will think above all of the likelihood of being caught; but he will also consider whether being caught is likely to lead to a prison sentence or a mere non-custodial sentence; and if a prison sentence seems likely he may even wonder how long it will be. All of which is closer to common-sense beliefs than the exaggerated doctrine that only the likelihood of being caught deters or fails to deter.

What has been said so far applies to 'crimes': robberies, rapes, other forms of violence, burglaries. We know less about the ways in which people are deterred from committing less serious 'offences'. Since clear-up-rates for these are either unpublished or misleading,[18] people's estimates of risk have to be ascertained by interviewing samples, who must also be asked how often they commit the offence in question—a somewhat artificial situation. The usual finding, however, is that low estimates of risk are associated with high or fairly high frequencies of offending, and vice versa. It is the part played by the penalties that is less certain. Usually they are fines, either of standard sums or of an amount which the offender is deemed able to pay without undue hardship; so that it is not possible to tell what effect more severe or more lenient penalties would have. We do know that where parking fines were replaced by wheel-clamping—for example in certain parts of central London—illegal parking decreased sharply.[19] As for driving offences, it is disqualification, not fines, which motorists are most anxious to avoid. There have also been a few interview-studies in which self-reported delinquencies—such as marijuana use in the United States—varied inversely with the severity of the penalty expected by respondents.

Yet even where non-custodial penalties for petty offences are concerned, it is very difficult to argue convincingly that the notion of a sufficient penalty plays no part in deterrence. It is reasonable to hypothesize that variations in the subjective probability of detection have more effect than variations in the amount of a fine or the duration of a community service order; and if true this has important implications for policy. It is almost certainly true also that in the case of most petty offences there are people who refrain solely because they fear detection or public prosecution, and not because a fine would incommode them. What is quite implausible, and supported by no evidence whatsoever, is to claim that this is true of all potential perpetrators of any kind of petty offence. And if we consider offences which do not stigmatize—for example, illegal parking—it becomes obvious that not only the existence of a penalty but also its nature play a part in deterrence. There are motorists, as we have seen, who are not deterred by fines but for whom wheel-clamping is the 'sufficient deterrent'.

Many other points could be elicited from the voluminous literature on deterrence. I have selected only what seems relevant to the question 'Is the nature of the penalty a negligible or an important consideration when people in deterrable states of mind are thinking of breaking the law?' Common sense says that it is not negligible. Most of the evidence is consistent with common sense.

iv. The sentencer's dilemma

There remains, however, the sentencer's dilemma to be considered. He is often faced with an offender for whom the normal penalty would be a prison sentence, but whom, for one reason or another, he wants merely to fine or put on probation. Will this weaken the deterrent effect? In most cases his decision will receive no publicity, and will merely contribute a digit to statistics which are studied only by statisticians. (Of course if the offender is a well-known personality, or if the crime itself has attracted publicity, the news media will be paying attention; but that is not the sort of case at issue.) Is there any reason why he should not be lenient? There is. Leniency itself is apt to attract publicity. Unless he can give a public explanation of a kind which the news media will understand and present as acceptable, he is likely to be pilloried. The result may be to give the impression that anyone who commits a similar offence but has a good lawyer and favourable reports from social workers or psychiatrists can expect the same clemency. Situations of this kind are common in sentencers' experience, and face them with decisions that are far from easy.

Suppose, on the other hand, that the sentencer is minded to 'make an example' of the offender, and impose a more severe sentence than is usual. Sometimes he can justify this on the ground that the crime was 'aggravated' by special features:

sadistic cruelty, careful premeditation, or a history of previous crimes of a similar kind. Sometimes, however, he simply reasons that crimes of this kind have become too frequent, and he must reinforce deterrence with a particularly severe penalty. Do 'exemplary' sentences have this effect? I know of only one attempt to measure it. In 1973 a Birmingham youth was sentenced to twenty years' detention for a particularly brutal mugging. This quite exceptional sentence received a lot of publicity in local and national newspapers. Later, two researchers[20] studied the week-by-week frequencies of muggings *before and after* the sentence, in Liverpool and Manchester as well as Birmingham. They could find no sign of a decrease. Perhaps too few muggers read newspapers. One negative finding of this kind, of course, does not show that there is no sort of offence which can be discouraged by exemplary sentencing. Financiers, for instance, study the news more often than muggers do. When they are convicted, their prison sentences are usually short, but with an occasional exception of an exemplary length. Financial offences seem to be as frequent as ever. But nobody has achieved a similar comparison of a statistical kind.

So much for the criticism of general deterrence which is based on the assertion that the choice of penalty is not an important factor. There remains the objection that sentencing one person in order to deter others is making use of him in an immoral way; this will be discussed in Chapter 6.

3

Educating or Satisfying Others

WHATEVER one's beliefs about the efficacy of deterrents, it is possible to credit penalties with other useful effects on the public: educating it, or at least satisfying it. For the moment consider the possibility of an educative effect. The idea is not new. Early in the eighteenth century an English lawyer Sollum Emlyn argued that 'the lower part of mankind' judged the heinousness of offences by the severity of the punishment, so that the use of capital punishment for a wide range of offences made them less able to distinguish 'extraordinary guilt'.[1] A generation later the Italian utilitarian Cesare Beccaria made the same point.[2]

Bentham's interest was in deterrence, and neither he nor his followers took much interest in Sollum Emlyn's notion. It was the nineteenth-century judge Fitzjames Stephen who gave it respectability in Victorian discourse. His often-quoted passage will bear one more repetition:

Great part of the general detestation of crime which happily prevails among the decent part of the community in all civilised countries arises from the fact that the commission of offences is associated in all such communities with the solemn and deliberate infliction of punishment whenever crime is proved . . . I think it highly desirable that criminals should be hated, that the punishments inflicted upon them should be so contrived as to give expression to that hatred and to justify it.[3]

Stephen did not regard this as the only function of punishment, and certainly not as its main justification. Ten years later, however, the French sociologist Durkheim went further, arguing that it

does not serve, or only quite secondarily, in correcting the culpable or in intimidating possible followers . . . Its true function is to maintain social cohesion intact . . . Denied so categorically, it would necessarily lose its energy, if an emotional reaction did not come to compensate its loss . . . and the only means of affirming it is to express the unanimous aversion which the crime continues to inspire, by an authentic act which can consist only in suffering inflicted upon the agent . . . [4]

But it was the English judges to whom the idea appealed most strongly, and for Lord Denning, giving what is called 'evidence' to the Gowers Commission, it was 'the ultimate justification' of the death penalty.[5] A few years later the Law Society's 'evidence' to another Commission invented the 'D Factor'— the expression of 'disapprobation' by means of punishment, although like many English judges they regarded it as 'an aspect of retribution'.[6]

i. The theory in the courts

By the middle of the 1960s it was appearing in the dicta of the Court of Criminal Appeal and the Court of Appeal (Criminal Division), first in *R.* v. *Llewellyn-Jones*[7] but more spectacularly in *R.* v. *Sargeant.*[8]

I will start with retribution. The Old Testament concept of an eye for an eye and a tooth for a tooth no longer plays any part in our criminal law. There is however another aspect of retribution . . . it is that society, through the courts must show its abhorrence of particular types of crime . . . The courts do not have to reflect public opinion. On the other hand the courts must not disregard it. Perhaps the main duty of the court is to *lead* public opinion.

Note again the way in which the symbolic function is called an 'aspect of retribution': a point to which I shall return in Chapter 9.

Lord Denning's 'ultimate justification' of capital punishment cut less ice in the United States. The Supreme Court's discussion of the arguments for and against the death penalty (in *Gregg* v. *Georgia* (1976)) relegated it to a footnote. Mr Justice Marshall's dissenting opinion paid it more attention, but only in order to reject it:

It is inconceivable that any individual concerned about conforming his conduct to what society says is 'right' would fail to realise that murder is 'wrong' if the penalty were simply life imprisonment.

ii. Moral philosophers

Nor were English moral philosophers as enthusiastic as Durkheim or Denning. Rashdall,[9] Bosanquet,[10] and Ewing[11] saw the denouncing of crime by punishment as one of its salutary functions, but not as its 'true function' or 'ultimate justification'. It was not until 1965 that a philosopher in the United States devoted a whole monograph to 'The Expressive Function of Punishment'.[12] He pointed out four ways in which it functioned:

1. *Authoritative disavowal.* It is common international practice, he said, for a country which believes that its rights have been violated by an agent of another country to ask that country to punish him. By doing so that country disavows the violation.

2. *Symbolic non-acquiescence.* Kant believed that even if a community were about to be disbanded or destroyed it should first execute the last murderer left in its jails, 'for otherwise the members of the community might be regarded as participators in the murder...'(1797). Similarly, says Feinberg, even those who disapprove of hating criminals and of the harshness of penal laws are likely to protest if certain kinds of behaviour are allowed to go unpunished: his example is the Texas law which completely excused a husband who killed a wife for adultery, a provision which Feinberg regards as abhorrent.

3. *Vindication of the law.* If the criminal law forbids something, then to leave unpunished a person who has infringed it 'gives rise to doubts that the law really means what it says', according to Feinberg. We shall see how this point has been developed by Hyman Gross.

4. *Absolution of others.* Feinberg argues that 'when something scandalous has occurred and it is clear that the wrongdoer must be one of a small number of suspects, then the state, by punishing one of these parties thereby relieves the others of suspicion and informally absolves them of blame'.

This list is far from satisfying. In the first place, Feinberg fails to distinguish sufficiently the transactions of convicting and sentencing. In the examples which he uses to illustrate his last function—the absolution of others—it would be achieved by convicting the wrongdoers. It is true that the expressive effect of the conviction would be greatly weakened if the conviction were not followed by a punitive sentence; but it is the declaration of guilt which seems to be essential to achieve this function. As for his first two functions—disavowal and symbolic non-acquiescence—three points must be made about them. First, they are not really distinguishable: disavowal seems simply to be a special case of symbolic non-acquiescence. Secondly, the attitude of Texas law towards homicide provoked by adultery is an odd choice of example. All it illustrates is that excuses approved by one culture may be disapproved by others. It has nothing to do with the function of punishment. A better example would have been the extremely mild penalties imposed on, say, people who drive when drunk, which are often interpreted as signs of tolerance.

Thirdly, the choice of such out-of-the-way examples betrays the fact that it is only in certain circumstances, and not regularly, that sentences function expressively. This is indeed Feinberg's view: he makes it clear that he does not really believe that all sentences function in this way. Moreover, he distinguishes 'penalties'—such as fines—for regulatory offences from 'punishments'—usually of more severe kinds—for crimes; and it is only the latter which in his view have a 'reprobative' function. It is difficult, however, to see why symbolic non-acquiescence in, say, drunken driving should not be expressed by means of a fine. No doubt a fine is a less emphatic symbol than a prison sentence; but a really heavy fine can be quite dramatic: witness the publicity given by the news media to the large fines imposed by English magistrates for smuggling pets which might carry rabies into the country, and the equally startling fines (of £1,000) imposed on some foreign tourists for shop-lifting.

iii. Anti-impunity

More important, Feinberg does not assert that denunciation is 'the ultimate justification' for punishment. On the contrary, he talks of its relationship to the 'various central purposes' of punishment, by which he seems to mean deterrence, reform, and rehabilitation. It is Hyman Gross who argues in favour of a version of the expressive theory as the only tenable justification for penalties. It is true that he regards his version as a sophisticated version of deterrence; but it soon becomes clear that this is only because it stresses 'the threats made by the law'. His view is that

punishment for violating the rules of conduct laid down by the law is necessary if the law is to remain a sufficiently strong influence to keep the community on the whole law-abiding . . . Without punishment for violating these rules the law becomes merely a guide and an exhortation to right conduct . . . The threats of the criminal law are necessary, then, only as part of a system of liability ensuring that those who commit crimes do not get away with them. The threats are not laid down to deter those tempted to break the rules, but rather to maintain the rules as a set of standards that compel allegiance in spite of violations by those who commit crimes . . . there is punishment for violation of these rules in order to prevent the dissipation of their power that would result if they were violated with impunity.[13]

Like Feinberg, Gross is a utilitarian. His 'anti-impunity' function is very like Feinberg's 'vindication of the law'. The difference is that Gross sees it as the only sound justification for sentencing. It is true that his introductory chapter grants that desert, correction, and incapacitation have 'a proper place somewhere among the aims and purposes of criminal justice': but later in the book they are dismissed.

At the same time he is curiously influenced by retributive notions. For example, when he comes to what he calls 'the principle of mitigation of sentence' he does not really succeed in showing why it is a principle if his justification is the only sound one. Instead of acknowledging that any reduction of penalties in individual cases must be counter-productive, he feels obliged to argue that

If there is good reason for a lighter sentence than fits the crime, the heavier sentence in spite of that is unnecessary, and so it is unjustifiable punishment. This is so because no one would be deemed to have got away with his crime if under these circumstances he were given the lighter sentence. Condemnation for the crime would be no less.

If he had merely been arguing that retributive justice must be allowed to set limits to what is expedient by way of denunciation even if it thereby weakens it, he would have been compromising with retribution in the same way as most other utilitarians. But he is actually arguing that if there is a good (retributive) reason for a lighter sentence then it does *not* weaken the expressive effect. This would be true only if everyone who knew about the lighter penalty understood and agreed with the sentencer's reasons for choosing it. In real life it just does not happen that way: judges who deal with robbers, rapists, and other serious offenders by means of suspended sentences, fines, or probation provoke storms of protest from newspapers and readers who either were not told the reasons for such leniency or do not accept them. As I have hinted, however, Gross could have avoided this pitfall, either by asserting boldly that mitigation of penalties was ruled out by his justification or by confessing that he was compromising: that is, accepting limits set by retribution, even when they weaken denunciation.

This point illustrates a tendency shared by most exponents of denunciation: a failure to take into account the facts of life. The expressive theory—at least in its instrumental version—treats penalties as a means whereby an assertion (e.g. that rules are not flouted with impunity) is communicated to people who might flout them. Yet it is common knowledge, especially amongst potential offenders, that huge numbers of offences are *not* punished. Are the occasions on which they *are* punished supposed to be numerous enough to make people forget this? It is a very small percentage of sentences which is reported in the news media. National newspapers, radio, and television are very selective, reporting only offences which are in some way unusual, or which involve well-known names. Local newpapers are less selective, and often use short reports of sentences for quite ordinary offences to fill in the spaces between national news and advertisements. It is these reports, if anything, which give some degree of realism to the expressive theory. Statistics of sentences cannot do so. Even if they were read by the lay public (which they are not), what would strike the reader would be the figures which show offenders being discharged, put on probation, or receiving suspended sentences for crimes such as manslaughter, causing death by dangerous driving, rape, robbery: figures which are not accompanied by any of the special reasoning that must have led to such disposals.[14]

It is true, as we have seen, that occasionally these lenient sentences are publicized, and lead to protests. It is possible that they do weaken respect for the rules which the offenders have infringed; and I have therefore argued that the consistent denouncer should be opposed to leniency, however desirable for other reasons. In fact, there is no evidence for or against this assumption. For all we know, the public criticism provoked by Mr Justice Humphrey's suspended sentence for a multiple rapist[15] strengthened rather than undermined the social cohesion on the subject on which Durkheim laid so much emphasis. Nevertheless, so many sentencers believe that in some way they are maintaining moral standards by strict sentences that it would be useful to have empirical evidence on the soundness of this belief.

iv. Empirical evidence

The only relevant empirical study known to me is one which I carried out myself with the help of Catherine Marsh, an expert in survey methods.[16] Using professional interviewers, we showed some 1,200 adults faked newspaper cuttings describing six different incidents which involved moderately serious offences. The stories did not include the sentence, because we were experimenting to see whether this affected our respondents' disapproval of the offence. Randomized subsamples were then given one of six additional pieces of information: (1) that the offender had been imprisoned for six months; or (2) that he had been put on probation; or (3) that the judge said that he took a serious view of this sort of case; or (4) that the judge said he did not take a serious view of it; or (5) that most 'people like yourself' do not disapprove much of what the offender did; or (6) that most 'people like yourself' disapprove strongly of it. Respondents were then asked to indicate the degree of their own disapproval on a seven-point scale.[17] The most important finding was that varying the sentence from six months' imprisonment to probation made no significant difference to their mean disapproval scores. Nor did the information about the judge's disapproval. Yet telling them what 'people like yourself' felt about the offence did make a significant difference. In short, it is possible to influence people's disapproval by that sort of information, but not by means of information about severe or lenient sentencing.

A possibility which we could not, of course, exclude was that disapproval of moderately serious offences might be influenced not by a newspaper report of a single case but by a series of reported sentences of a consistently lenient or severe kind. In real life, however, it is not series of consistent sentences that make news, but unusual features of individual cases (a recent example was 'HUNGARIAN TIGHT-ROPE WALKER WITH BROKEN LEGS DRANK AND DROVE'). Long-drawn-out messages consisting of regular sentences over extended periods never reach the public. The Court of Appeal's belief in 'the Sargeant effect' seems a forlorn hope.

v. Other beneficiaries?

This does not dispose completely of the instrumental version of the denunciatory theory. We have to consider two points made by Sir Walter Moberly. He was not primarily a denouncer: he cannot be labelled as anything but an eclectic.[18] But he was influenced by Bosanquet, and believed that amongst the purposes of punishment was its symbolic effect on the wrong-doer—and the punisher—as well as on the public at large:

Persons in authority then will punish wrongdoers because they detest wrongdoing, appreciate its ruinous character and are determined to withstand and overcome it. They will desire (1) to deepen and consolidate this attitude in themselves, (2) to promulgate it to the world, (3) to bring it home to the apprehension of the evildoer. These aims are properly inseparable, and each is indispensable.

What he meant by the 'ruinous character' of wrongdoing was the moral deterioration which takes place if the wrongdoer does not repent. The suffering imposed by punishment is supposed to stimulate appreciation of this by its symbolism. What is symbolized is complex: a combination of both 'the consumma-tion and the annulment of wrong'.

Moberly was not as sceptical as perhaps he should have been about the symbolic effect of punishment on 'the world'; and his ideas are firmly based on the notion of the moral deterioration entailed by unrepentant sinning. What is of interest, however, and perhaps of value, is his claim that punishment has a beneficial symbolic effect on both the punishing authority and the punished offender. I have cast doubt on the assumption that news about punishments reaches enough members of 'the world' to make the transaction worthwhile. By contrast, there can be no doubt that each punishment is known both to the punishing authority (at least if that means the sentencer) and to the person punished.

What is more, there is a high degree of armchair credibility, to say the least, about the assertion that the act of ordering punishment 'consolidates' whatever attitude the sentencer may have towards the wrongdoing for which the punishment is awarded, *whether or not he shares Moberly's views*. In plain terms, the assertion is that each occasion on which a sentencer awards an unchallenged sentence for an offence of a given type makes it less likely that he will be persuaded in the future to take a lenient view of that type of offence. (It seems necessary to add the gloss 'unchallenged' since a successful appeal against a sentence, or even public or private criticism of it, might have a contrary effect.) Whether it is always desirable that sentencers should reinforce their own censoriousness in this way is another question.

Moberly's third hope—that the penalty would bring home the detestability of the offence to the offender himself—has been developed by Duff[19] and others into a full-blown justification for sentencing; but the proper place for a discussion of this is in the chapter on the justification of retribution (Chapter 9).

vi. The ritual version

So much for the utilitarian version of the expressive theory. It is not the only one. If the Canadian Law Reform Commission is to be understood literally, theirs is a non-utilitarian version:

Organising the future . . . is not the major function of the criminal law. Even if we cannot control the future, this does not mean we must ignore the present and the past. We still need to do something about wrongful acts; to register our social disapproval, to publicly denounce them and to reaffirm the values violated by them.[20]

If the Commission really meant that denunciation has regard to 'the present and the past' and that 'Organising the future' is not its function, this is a non-utilitarian justification. It is by no means impossible that this is what they meant. In the minds of some judges—and other people who think hard about law-breaking—denunciation is closely linked with the retributive justification. Lord Justice Lawton's remarks in *R*. v. *Sargeant*—quoted earlier—showed that he regarded denunciation as an aspect of retribution—a more sophisticated version of it than the *lex talionis*. In *R*. v. *Llewellyn-Jones* the Court of Appeal (per Lord Parker CJ) said that a four-year prison sentence for dishonest conversion of funds was 'a sentence which is fully merited . . . as a punishment for very grave offences, and as *expressing the revulsion of the public* to the whole circumstances of the case'.[21] In this version denunciation is not leading public opinion, it is expressing it. A similar version seems to have been in the mind of the Archbishop of York in the 1965 debate in the House of Lords on capital punishment:

society must say, through its officers of law, that it repudiates certain acts as utterly incompatible with civilised conduct and that it will exact retribution from those who violate its ordered code.[22]

For him, too, denunciation was an aspect of retribution, and an expression not merely of the sentencer's disapproval but of society's.

There does then seem to be, at least in the minds of some people who think a lot about punishment, a non-utilitarian version of the expressive justification. The fact that it can be linked—even confused—with retribution, so as to be called an aspect of it, underlines its non-utilitarian nature, and requires a little consideration.

Denunciation certainly resembles retribution to the extent that both are responses to a past act; and like retribution it can be regarded as having no designs on the future. On the other hand, the two justifications differ in an important way. The retributivist must logically demand that the punishment actually be inflicted; but the denouncer need not. So long as the sentence is pronounced and people believe that it will be carried out, disapproval has been expressed. It should not matter if secretly the offender is smuggled away from the Old Bailey under another name to live in freedom on the Costa Brava.[23] The retributive justification entails genuine infliction of penalties: denunciation merely requires that people believe in the infliction. This is also true, incidentally, of the instrumental version: but that is less easily confused with retribution, although, as I have shown, it can be done.

This being so, what non-utilitarian denouncers seem to have in mind is a ritual expression of disapproval. Its point must lie not in its effect on future behaviour but in the immediate satisfaction derived from the act of expression, just as the point of a memorial service lies in the expression of respect or affection for the dead. The fact that the dead need not be present, and that the offender need not actually be punished (in theory at least), is all the more reason for regarding the term 'ritual' as very appropriate.

But there are questions to be answered. Who is being satisfied, for example? No doubt some of the participants in the ritual: the sentencer himself, the prosecutor, the victim and his sympathizers in the gallery. True, most trials, like most funerals, are poorly attended; but in a special selection of cases participation is extended to a wider audience by the news media. So perhaps ritual denouncers can claim to be satisfying the public?

If so, a fair question is 'What do we know about the extent to which the public derives satisfaction from what it is told about sentences or sentencing?' Again, answers from the armchair are not to be trusted. Opinion surveys at least tell us what interviewees tell interviewers. Satisfaction, it is true, is notoriously hard to measure. It is not a mere absence of dissatisfaction. Nor is it mere agreement with abstract statements about the aims of sentencing. If it is to be any sort of justification for a ritual view of sentencing it must be a positive feeling that in a specific case or type of case the sentencer has struck the right note. I do not know of any opinion survey that has attempted to identify this feeling.

Some survey questions, however, have yielded findings which make it rather unlikely that positive satisfaction is the reaction of most of the public. For instance, in the Walker–Marsh survey just described, respondents were asked what penalty they thought the offender *should have* got, and then what they thought he actually *did* get. The percentages which expected him to get what they thought right varied for each type of offence (a reassuring indication that they were not responding unthinkingly); but in each case very substantial percentages— and in one case a majority—expected the sentencer's penalty to be more severe or lenient than the one they would have chosen. These respondents were clearly cynical rather than satisfied with what they had learned about sentencing. From other surveys[24] we know that many respondents underestimate the percentages of, say, convicted burglars who are sent to prison (it is in fact about 50 per cent). When asked 'What do you think of the sentences that courts generally give for rape?', 90 per cent of English subjects chose 'too soft'; and 87 per cent said the same of mugging. For the less serious offence of shop-lifting a bare majority chose 'about right'.

These responses of course reflect the impressions which respondents derive from the news media. Newspapers, radio, and television pay more attention to the details of offences than to sentences, and tend to highlight the latter only when they can be presented as too lenient or—sometimes—too severe. This means that the more attention a member of the public pays to news about crime the more likely he is to be *dissatisfied* with sentences. For believers in ritual denunciation this is extremely awkward.

Finally, we must not overlook the likelihood that some sentences have effects which are neither moral education nor ritual satisfaction, but something quite undesirable. We have seen that in some types of case substantial percentages of respondents regarded the sentence as too lenient or severe. It may well be the case—as Canadian experiments suggest[25]— that these percentages would be smaller if the public had been given more of the information which the sentencer had been given. But that is beside the point. What is to the point is that the way in which the news media present sentences is likely to foster cynicism rather than confidence about law-enforcement. In some cases the effect may even be a backlash of antagonism, especially if the news media present the offender as particularly deserving of sympathy or condemnation. This is not a refutation of expressive theories: merely another awkward fact which they must take into account.

Suppose, however, that a ritualist could find people who admit to the positive sort of satisfaction for which he hopes. If they were asked why they experienced this satisfaction they would almost certainly give either retributive or utilitarian replies: that the offender deserves the sentence or that it will help to reduce law-breaking. It is highly unlikely that the ritualist would find any unsophisticated respondents who would reply to his question in ritual terms. This is not a fatal objection; but it does point to an important difference between sentencing and other rituals, in which the participants *are* satisfied for ritual reasons.

4

Elimination and Incapacitation

THE hard-headed man in the street is less interested in the educative or ritual function of sentencing—if indeed he has heard of them—than in its protective efficacy. He wants would-be predators deterred and those that are not deterred put away. For some crimes he would like them to be eliminated: humanely executed. Where moderately serious crimes are concerned he would settle for long periods of incarceration.

The efficacy of these penalties in protecting the public from offenders who have been identified and convicted cannot be denied. From this point of view the death penalty has no equal. Incarceration is not quite so effective. Prisoners can escape, occasionally from secure prisons and quite easily from open ones, although escapers do not usually commit serious crimes while on the run. Inside, some prisoners are a menace to staff and to others, who have the same right to be protected against them as the law-abiding public.[1] In any case, most prisoners' sentences are determinate, so that by a certain date they must be released; and in countries with parole systems many are even released before that date. Unless their sentences have been long enough to detain them until they are middle-aged or elderly, they are physically and mentally able to repeat their offences. In Britain three-quarters of custodial sentences are of eighteen months or less. If incarceration could be relied upon to correct most offenders such sentences might be regarded as a protection; but it cannot. So most sentences merely postpone opportunities for reoffending. Yet a judge's remark that the public needs protection against an offender is not infrequently the preface to a sentence which will mean his release after quite a short period.

i. Indeterminate sentences

Some penal codes, however, provide special indeterminate sentences for offenders who seem likely to repeat very harmful offences. Usually these sentences are discretionary, so that courts are not forced to use them; but sometimes they are mandatory. In Britain the 'life' sentence is mandatory for murder, discretionary for a number of other offences; and when it is discretionary, courts do not usually employ it unless satisfied that the offender's mental instability makes him likely to be dangerous for an unforeseeable period. 'Life' must be spelt with inverted commas because in most jurisdictions it does not mean what it says.[2] There is usually an assumption that a prisoner serving an indeterminate sentence will be released at some date, however distant. There comes a juncture in nearly every indeterminate sentence at which people begin to wonder whether the prisoner has not served long enough to meet the needs of general deterrence—or, if they are so minded, retribution. In the English parole system this point is explicitly fixed by Home Office ministers, who may specify ten, twelve, twenty, or more years. After that, the sole question for the Parole Board is supposed to be 'Is the risk of the prisoner's committing another grave offence low enough to allow us to recommend release on licence?' Since release from a 'life' sentence is conditional on good behaviour and compliance with requirements to keep in touch with a supervisor and to live at an approved address, the Board may be more optimistic about the risk than it would be if release were unconditional; but it may take the view that the offender is so impulsive or compulsive[3] that supervision would do nothing to prevent a repetition.[4]

A prisoner conditionally released, whether from a determinate or indeterminate sentence, can be recalled for any breach of his conditions. If his sentence was determinate his liability to recall expires at the date when he would have had to be released if not paroled. Lifers, however, are recallable until the end of their lives, even if the specific requirements of supervision have been allowed to lapse. If recalled, the prisoner has the right of appeal—in Britain to the Parole Board.

Indeterminacy makes release a politically sensitive matter. A determinate-sentence prisoner must by law be set free by a certain date, so that whatever crime he commits thereafter the officials who release him cannot be blamed for it. By contrast the minister, parole board, or official who decides that it is safe to release a murderer, rapist, or child-molester from an indeterminate sentence is usually held responsible by the news media if the ex-prisoner commits another crime of the same sort. Even the news of the release may give rise to furious criticism if the original crime was sufficiently horrific. Most prison systems hold inmates whom the authorities hesitate to discharge for political reasons,[5] even after decades of confinement have reduced their propensity for harm to a very low level.

ii. Practical problems

Yet long precautionary sentences create practical problems. They load prison systems with inmates who need special care. In England and Wales, for example, although only about two in every thousand prison sentences are for 'life', lifers remain inside for so much longer than other prisoners that they account for 6 per cent of the resident population.[6] The high security which some of them need is extremely costly, although those for whom release is just over the horizon are tested in the cheaper conditions of open prisons. Lifers with little hope of release in the foreseeable future can be hard to manage: ordinary prisoners fear loss of remission,[7] but lifers cannot be threatened with that. Some—fortunately not many—have to be segregated for the sake of peace and quiet. Prisoners serving very long determinate sentences can be equally difficult. Precautionary incarceration is the most expensive penalty ever invented.

Another problem is the welfare of long-term prisoners and their dependants. In modern penal theory imprisonment should not involve avoidable harm to them. The penalty is meant to be deprivation of freedom, not the infliction of additional hardship. Short-term detention seldom does lasting damage to the prisoner himself. Occasionally he is maimed by a fellow-prisoner, or contracts a serious infection (drug-injecting prisoners are at risk of hepatitis or AIDS, for example). But so long as he behaves sensibly, and is fed and exercised as the rules require, he will usually emerge none the worse.[8] It is his wife and children—if he has been a good husband and father—who are likely to suffer:[9] a problem discussed in Chapter 13.

What we are concerned with, however, are long-term inmates. They enjoy better conditions than overcrowded short-termers, and their physical deterioration is not greater than is to be expected with the passage of time, provided that they take opportunities for exercise. (Indeed some of them lead healthier lives inside.) It is their mental health which is the focus of anxiety. Incarceration does not of itself cause mental illness[10] unless conditions approximate to sensory deprivation. Nor does it cause low intelligence or personality disorder. Depression is, not surprisingly, frequent in the early months of a long sentence, and when hopes of parole are disappointed; but these are natural, not pathological, reactions. More realistic is anxiety about 'institutionalization'. Long-term prisoners—even those with foreseeable release-dates—gradually lose contact with relatives and friends outside. After six or seven years most wives and girlfriends have given them up, and their remaining visitors, if any, are usually their mothers. Their interests narrow, and they are preoccupied with prison gossip and one or two engrossing hobbies. Most decisions are taken for them by the rules, so that they lose initiative. This is one way of 'doing time' with the minimum of distress. A few fight the system, disobeying rules and conspiring against staff in serious or petty ways: another way of keeping alert. Some co-operate energetically, helping to staff the library, the gymnasium, or the officers' mess. Some resort to meditation, with or without the help of drugs.

Not all these modes of adaptation should be regarded as unhealthy. The important question, however, is whether those that seem undesirable are permanent or transitory. Does 'institutionalization' persist after release? Surprising as it may seem, I cannot find any psychological study of *ex*-prisoners which addresses itself to this question. The nearest thing to good evidence is John Coker's follow-up of 239 lifers who had been released after long periods in prison. Although most of them were from 'the lowest socio-economic group and poorly educated'—whom one would therefore expect to be most vulnerable—he found that

These men showed no evidence of deterioration as a result of their long years in prison . . . In general, after a short period of resettlement,

sometimes accompanied by restlessness, they obtained and kept work
and accommodation . . . and many married or remarried and made
new homes. In some cases men improved upon their previous levels
of employment. Additionally these lifers revealed, generally, a fierce
desire for independence and a capacity to manage their own lives
competently . . . [11]

In short, 'institutionalization' is either rare or, if common,
reversible.

By exaggerating the side-effects of long imprisonment, penal
reformers have distracted attention from the undeniable harm
which it does: the deprivation of freedom for what are usually
the best parts of people's lives.[12] It is this which needs a
convincing justification, at least in societies which are normally
content with fairly short custodial sentences. Where long
sentences are the norm, either because they are thought
necessary to deter or because they are regarded as deserved,
the precautionary justification is seldom discussed: the protection of the public is simply a welcome by-product. It is when
sentences become shorter that a need is felt for the detention of
some offenders for exceptionally long periods.

iii. Anti-protectionists

To the hard-headed man in the street the utilitarian justification
seems obvious. The longer a murderer, rapist, child-molester,
or armed robber is detained the fewer the people he will
victimize in the future: hopefully none. There are anti-
protectionists, however, who do not accept this justification.
They can be distinguished:

1. Some hold that nothing can justify the detention of
   anyone for a longer period than he *deserves*. (They might
   make exceptions for cases in which moderate extensions
   would allow the completion of treatment which is clearly
   beneficial to the detainee: for example medical or
   psychiatric treatment; but that is not the point here.) An
   example is a Swedish committee; and their argument is
   discussed in Chapter 8.
2. A less extreme position accepts the detention of offenders
   who have done grave harm to others and seem certain—

barring unforeseeable events such as death or disablement—to do further grave harm if set free; but argues that such cases are very rare,[13] and that even offenders who have done grave harm more than once are far from certain to do it again. This being so, a policy which detains them for longer than would an ordinary sentence involves *mistakes*, and mistakes which inflict serious harm on the detainees. The argument implies that mistakes of this sort are immoral. Like the argument based on desert, it will therefore be discussed in Part II, along with other moral objections.

Meanwhile we must notice another anti-protectionist point: that a policy which detains for the sake of prevention in fact makes only a very small contribution to the protection of the public. Most murders, rapes, and so forth are committed by people who have not been detected in previous offending, or at least not in anything worse than dishonesty or traffic offences. If those whose crimes inflicted grave harm were simply given sentences commensurate with the harm, the argument goes, the crimes they committed after release would make a negligible addition to the volume of really harmful crimes.

A lot seems to depend, however, on how the contribution is estimated, and whether the result is regarded as 'negligible'. Researchers in the United States—but not so far in Britain—have tried various methods of calculation. One of the difficulties is that while it is easy to identify crimes that could have been prevented by longer detention when those crimes have been traced to people with previous convictions, it is far from easy in the case of unsolved crimes; and these are numerous. No doubt some of the unsolved crimes were committed by people released from sentences for similar crimes, and some by people who had not served custodial sentences: but in what proportions? The best study so far is probably one by Greenwood and Abrahamse.[14] Using self-reports and other information about the careers of robbers and some other kinds of criminal in Californian and Texan penitentiaries they estimated that something like a 15 per cent reduction in California's robberies could be achieved by identifying 'high-rate robbers' and lengthening their sentences. It cannot be assumed, of course, that equal gains could be achieved in every jurisdiction, or for every sort of serious crime. In Texas, where sentences were longer and robbery-rates lower, the estimated gain was smaller.[15] But this piece of research makes it implausible to argue that the contribution made by policies of precautionary detention is 'negligible'.

A hard-headed economist might concede that the contribution is more than 'negligible' but argue that the cost of keeping, say, high-rate robbers in prisons for greatly lengthened periods would—or might—exceed the cost of their depredations. Comparative estimates would depend on the definition of 'high-rate' and of the cost.[16] Whatever the result of such a calculation, it would have to be a very hard-headed economist who would extend the argument to crimes such as homicide, rape, or child-molesting. Victims of such crimes, or their relatives, can be compensated financially, and are compensated in some jurisdictions; but however generous the compensation few would choose to be victimized and compensated.

It is interesting that anti-protectionists do not raise similar objections to non-custodial forms of precautionary sentencing: to disqualification from driving, or prohibitions from engaging in certain occupations.[17] The reason must be that these do not greatly restrict the offender's freedom. The disqualified driver can get drunk with impunity, so long as he does not become disorderly or violent. The ex-teacher can find another occupation.[18] In Britain it is only curfews and electronic surveillance that are regarded as objectionable, by many people at least. Even the National Association of Probation Officers is amongst the objectors. The main objection is not the difficulty of enforcement (which also applies to such measures as disqualification from driving), but the assumption that an offender who is not incarcerated is entitled to the same freedom as law-abiding citizens: an assumption which needs more discussion than it has received.

Whatever form precautionary measures take, however, they involve the same question of principle. An offender who has shown himself capable of committing an offence is, at least in the actuarial[19] sense, more likely to commit another one than someone who has not. 'Nothing predicts behaviour like behaviour',[20] even if its predictions are often wrong. Does merely enhanced probability justify us in imposing irksome restraints in order to reduce it? The Swedish committee would have to say 'No', although it is doubtful whether they meant their argument to apply to non-custodial restraints. However that may be, their reasoning conceals more than rhetorical sleight of hand, as we shall see in Chapter 8. Meanwhile one more utilitarian objective remains to be considered: the correction of offenders.

5

Correction

'CORRECTION' is a non-committal word, very wisely adopted
by penologists in the United States. When an offender who has
been penalized ceases to offend, it is often hard to be sure why.
The stigma of being labelled a thief or a mugger may have
decided him to show that he does not deserve the label.[1] The
unpleasant memory of the penalty may discourage him ('individual deterrence'). A parent or social worker may have
reasoned with him and persuaded him that his behaviour was
selfishly harmful to others ('reform'). A supervisor may have
found him employment or at least some law-abiding activity to
pass the time ('rehabilitation'[2]). Two or more of these processes
may have combined to produce the effect. To avoid begging an
important question it is safer to refer to the offender as
'corrected'.

Since this chapter is about penalties, the all-important
question is 'How often do they result in correction?' Only if the
answer proves to be 'quite often' or at least 'not infrequently' is
it worth investigating whether the correction is the result of
deterrence, reform, or rehabilitation. There was a time when
penologists would have replied 'quite often'. Their follow-ups
of ex-probationers or ex-inmates of reformative institutions
seemed to show that substantial percentages were 'successes', at
least in the sense that they had not been reconvicted (or
rearrested, the traditional American criterion). Later came the
realization that we did not know how many would have turned
out to be 'successes' if they had been dealt with otherwise, or
not at all. This milestone was reached when the famous
Cambridge–Somerville Youth Study followed up nearly 2,000
boys, half of whom had been assigned to counsellors, half
not. The researchers concluded that 'the special work of the
counsellors was no more effective than the usual forces in the
community in preventing boys from committing delinquent
acts'.[3] (What was not emphasized was that most of the

counsellors were untrained and inexperienced.) The importance of the study was that it put an end to optimistic
assessments of corrective efficacy which made no use of
'controls'.

Another belated realization was that follow-ups which
classified offenders as 'successes' ignored the very real possibility that they had reoffended without being detected.[4]
Most samples of offenders, whether adult or juvenile, on probation or in custody, are there because they have committed
petty acquisitive dishonesties, of the kind which have a low
clear-up-rate. It is therefore quite likely that some of them
will be mistakenly classified as successes in follow-ups which
rely on reconvictions.

This does not mean, however, that follow-ups of this kind are
completely misleading. They may not count successes, but they
do count known failures. And known-failure-rates seem to obey
certain laws of nature which suggest that follow-ups are
measuring something of value, however inaccurately. Males are
more likely to be failures than females. Amongst offenders of
the same sex, teenagers are more likely to fail than their elders:
recidivism declines with age, though after the teens the decline
is gradual. Amongst offenders of the same sex and age-group,
the more previous findings of guilt recorded against them the
more likely they are to incur subsequent findings. Amongst
adult males (at least), the unemployed are more likely to be
reconvicted than the employed. Some types of offence, too,
seem to be more repetitious than others. Thieves and burglars
are more likely to be reconvicted than men of violence, for
example, although there are of course *some* men whose records
show that they are prone to violence.

What this means is not that follow-up studies are invariably
misleading: only that they may be misleading if they do not
allow for the fact that the followed-up samples include
offenders with different reconviction probabilities. Allowance
can be made in one of two ways. At the stage at which offenders
are allotted to different sorts of treatment the allocation can be
deliberately random. This is hard to arrange, because there are
usually ethical and political objections. Courts are not usually
willing to do this.[5] Normally researchers have to rely on the
fact that courts' choices of sentence are *partially* random, in the

sense that they are *to some extent* governed by considerations which are *not* related to offenders' reconviction probabilities. This makes it possible for researchers to use statistical techniques to allow for the different reconviction percentages which are to be expected in the different samples.[6]

i. Comparisons of efficacy

This makes possible rough *comparisons* of the corrective efficacy of different types of sentence, but not estimates of their *absolute* efficacy. This could be achieved only if research could include suitable control samples of unsentenced offenders. At first sight they could use those who had been 'discharged' without penalty (or the equivalent in other jurisdictions). But their cases have special features: the triviality of the offence, the youth, old age, or illness of the offender, and other exceptional mitigating circumstances. Better would be a control sample of those who receive a suspended sentence of imprisonment: that is, a mere threat to impose it in the event of a subsequent conviction. Since this is a sentence of sorts, comparing the results with those of actual imprisonment can strictly speaking yield only an indication of comparative efficacy. Let us look for a moment, however, at the findings of a six-year follow-up of a large sample of males sentenced in England and Wales in January 1972. Reconviction-rates for actual imprisonment were markedly better than for suspended sentences.[7] The difference was most marked in the case of men convicted for the first time. Strictly speaking, all that this tells us is that the suspended sentence is less effective than an actual prison sentence. It is theoretically possible that the absolute efficacy of an actual prison sentence is nil (or even a minus quantity) and that the absolute efficacy of a suspended sentence is even less: that is, that it *increases* the likelihood of reconviction. The more likely explanation, however, is the common-sense one: that the memory of an actual prison sentence deters more offenders than the mere threat of one. There is independent evidence that the longer a prisoner spends inside, the less likely he is to be reconvicted.[8]

Deterrence, too, is the only possible explanation when a fine corrects an offender. Unfortunately we have virtually no evidence to tell us how often that happens. The six-year follow-up which I have described earlier did not include the kinds of traffic or regulatory offences which most often lead to fines: only 'standard list offences'. So far as adult men were concerned it showed that reconviction-rates after fines were roughly the same as the expected rates for the whole sample: neither markedly better nor markedly worse than those for imprisonment. The British fining system, however, was not designed to make the fine really effective as a deterrent, because of the half-hearted way in which the fine was adjusted to the offender's means. Courts had standard amounts in mind for different offences. They were prepared to reduce those amounts when satisfied that the offender was unable to find the money, or unable to do so without great hardship. But when the opposite was the case, and the offender was clearly able to pay the standard amount without the slightest inconvenience, they were not supposed to increase it. This paradoxical approach seemed almost intended to minimize the success of fines in achieving their only possible objective. It is only recently that English courts have been allowed to experiment with the Continental 'day-fine' system, in which the amount of the fine is closely related to the offender's income.

Consider now a measure which is intended not to deter but to reform or rehabilitate: probation. Every probation officer can recall offenders whom he has managed to keep 'out of trouble', at least while they were under his supervision; and only a bigoted sceptic would seriously maintain that this never happens. Unfortunately, aggregate statistics suggest that it is not the usual experience; and in any case that, after the period of supervision is over, some of the apparent 'successes' are reconvicted (as certainly happened in the six-year follow-up which I have just described).[9] True, ordinary probation, involving weekly meetings with a supervisor who tries to 'advise, assist and befriend',[10] is not a very intense experience, as both offenders and supervisors would agree. Yet even when probation was 'intensified' for randomly selected young offenders, as it was in the English IMPACT experiment,[11] their reconviction-rates were no better than those of the controls who had been subject to ordinary probation.

Probation, of course, is not the only useful activity of probation officers. They are responsible for organizing community service (whose corrective efficacy has yet to be thoroughly assessed). They run day-centres, which some probationers are required to attend, and thus are at least kept away for part of the day from opportunities for getting into trouble (day-centres may also provide constructive activities such as classes for illiterates or alcoholics). They supervise parolees. They provide sentencers—and defence lawyers— with 'social enquiry reports', outlining the offender's social background and history: these reports are often the only basis for counsel's plea in mitigation. They may even suggest the sort of sentence that would meet the case, although their tendency to suggest anything but a custodial sentence often discredits their reports. 'Advising, assisting and befriending', however, is much less often effective than sentencers are led to believe.[12]

Supervisory measures, however, allow the offender to remain in the social environment in which he misbehaved. Custody removes him from it, and makes it possible to subject him to less intermittent efforts. This is rarely practicable under ordinary prison conditions; but it has been attempted in special institutions for young offenders, with selected and trained staff. American states—notably California—have initiated many admirable experiments on these lines. Yet their findings have not pointed unequivocally to any sort of regime as being effective with the great mass of young offenders. Discouragement culminated in 1974, when Robert Martinson published an article based on a comprehensive review of the research literature in the English language. Entitled 'What Works?', it concluded that

With few and isolated exceptions, the rehabilitative efforts that have been reported so far have had no appreciable effect on recidivism.[13]

Other writers had said much the same,[14] but it was Martinson's article, in a semi-popular journal, which received wide publicity, and was interpreted as saying that the answer to his query was 'Nothing (much) works'. Before he died he tried to correct this impression, but only in an obscure law journal.[15]

ii. Identifying the corrigible

The controversy which followed served to highlight several important points. First, if an unselected—or randomly selected—

group of offenders is subjected to a measure or regime intended to reform, it is highly unlikely that it will have this effect on all of them. Not only will some be individuals who are unlikely to respond to any sort of corrective. Some will be of a kind who would have responded to some other sort of regime, but on whom the regime in question has the opposite effect to that intended. Concealed amongst these there may be individuals who do respond positively, but whose success is not evident in the aggregate follow-up figures, either because they were too few or because they were cancelled out, arithmetically speaking, by the failures of those who would have responded under a different regime. In California for instance, the Pilot Intensive Counselling Experiment found that the only offenders who seemed to respond positively were those who were 'bright, verbal and anxious'.[16] Other studies of this kind in the United States have defined likely improvers as YAVINS: young, anxious, verbal, intelligent, neurotic.

Another point is equally important. However carefully an offender is selected for a measure such as probation or a reformative custodial regime, the people to whom he is being entrusted will vary in their interpretation of what they are supposed to do to him. No two probation officers, even in the same office, handle their cases in the same way: even if they could they would protest against being expected to do so. No two institutions have exactly similar regimes; and even within the same institution no two staff members behave to inmates in exactly the same way. Consequently sentencers cannot prescribe standardized doses of probation, community service, or youth custody. Even the random allocation of subjects and controls to Measure A and Measure B can never be as rigorously scientific as administering Drug A and Placebo B to the subjects of pharmaceutical research.

iii. New ideas

These problems have to be faced whatever new approach to correction is proposed. For example, John Braithwaite advocates 'reintegrative shaming'.[17] Ways of dealing with offenders which stigmatize them, and alienate them from family or community, are unlikely to improve their conduct, and may even have the opposite effect. On the other hand procedures which allow the offender to express his regret, and be reaccepted by his law-abiding community, are beneficial and 'conscience-building'. Examples which he suggests are reparation and community service. His evidence is drawn not from any demonstration of the efficacy of these measures but mainly from his studies of white-collared offenders' reactions to adverse publicity, and from what he knows of Japanese ways of handling offenders (crime-rates in Japan are surprisingly low). His psychology is persuasive, but would be more so if he had acknowledged that his approach is more likely to succeed with young first-offenders from law-abiding families and small communities than with sophisticated criminals in large cities whose strongest ties are with people like themselves. Nor does he discuss the logistic difficulties of dealing reintegratively with large numbers of offenders. What this illustrates, however, is that the more general and unspecific the claims for a penological theory the more justified is scepticism.

iv. Mentally disordered offenders

So far I have ignored the mentally disordered. The state of the art is a little different where they are concerned. Their individual responses to treatment are more predictable than those of most normal offenders, at least when their law-breaking is clearly attributable to their disorder. Those who offend only when depressed, manic, or in epileptic states can be treated with drugs which reduce the likelihood of such episodes. The mentally impaired can sometimes be trained so that their social behaviour is less crude and objectionable. Abnormal jealousy sometimes responds to psychotherapy. Even schizophrenics may behave less alarmingly when the fears or rages which beset them are moderated by tranquillizing medicines. That said, there are many out-patients and in-patients about whom psychiatrists cannot be optimistic, and can predict only that they will sooner or later relapse, joining the stage army which reappears time and again in police stations, courts, prisons, and hospitals.

v. Scepticism

Special cases apart, however, what the evidence seems to say is that so far as reform and rehabilitation are concerned the sceptics have a good case, so long as they do not overstate it. 'Nothing works' is an overstatement. Some things work with some offenders, but not with most, or not for long. The minority who would respond to a specific measure, applied in a specific way, are not easily identified, even by professionals. Nor can anyone guarantee that a specific measure will be applied as the sentencer or professional adviser intended that it should be.

PART II
Moral Objections

PART I has dealt with one of the objections to utilitarian justifications for sentencing: that the declared aims of those justifications are not being attained, so that the suffering, hardship, or inconvenience which they impose on individuals are unjustifiable wrongs. What Part I must have demonstrated is that this is a considerable exaggeration. One objective is probably not being attained: the moral education of the public. And if sentencing is seen as a ritual it is one which is not satisfying a lot of people. Attempts to reform or rehabilitate offenders certainly have to contend with serious handicaps, and are often defeated, whether by the social environments to which offenders return, by their dispositions, or by lack of the expertise necessary for the selection of the right corrective. But this does not mean that they 'never work': only that we can seldom identify the cases in which they have worked, and so do not know how to maximize their frequency.

As for deterrence, the evidence does not support the claim that it doesn't work. Certainly fines, whose function can only be deterrent, do not seem very effective; but that is probably because fining systems seemed designed to minimize their effectiveness. Imprisonment, on the other hand, does seem, on the evidence, to deter some of those who experience it. The evidence also supports the common-sense belief that it deters some potential imitators who have not experienced it, provided that they are in deterrable states of mind. Indeed, the evidence seems to say that as a general deterrent the prospect of long imprisonment deters as many people from homicide as the death penalty does.

That does not dispose of the death penalty. As a deterrent it is cheaper than incarceration; and as a means of incapacitating dangerous offenders it is unequalled. When incapacitation,

however, is the main consideration, long indeterminate detention serves this purpose with enough efficiency to satisfy most
people. Admittedly it creates problems, as we saw in Chapter 5,
and especially when release has to be contemplated; but it is by
no means ineffective.

What Part I did not discuss were the moral objections to
penalties which are raised by people who are not necessarily
denying their effectiveness. The essence of these objections
is usually that penalties subject the offender to unpleasant,
damaging, or destructive experiences not for his sake (as
surgery or dentistry do) but for the sake of others. Sometimes
the moral objectors also draw attention to the possibility that
the penalty is being imposed *by mistake*: an argument which
is popular when the penalty in question is capital punishment
or precautionary detention. Consider first, however, the more
general argument that to penalize someone is to sacrifice him
to the interests of others.

6

Human Sacrifice?

THE argument is often attributed to Kant: but his objection to utilitarian aims was really of another kind. In his view the aim of penalties must be to inflict desert. This was a 'categorical imperative'. What that means will be considered in Chapter 9. Meanwhile it is important to recognize that he did not object to useful by-products of penalties. All he asserted was that 'one man ought never to be dealt with *merely* as a means subservient to the purposes of another . . .'. He disliked utilitarianism, particularly in the form advocated by Beccaria, but one reason for his dislike was that it seemed to point to *leniency*. His grim chapter on 'The Right of Punishing'[1] contains no objection to severity, or to the harm which penalties may inflict (he believed in equating the harm of the penalty to the harm of the crime). All he was claiming was that the categorical imperative to inflict what is deserved made other considerations irrelevant and sometimes misleading.

i. Using people

What needs to be distinguished from Kant's view is an objection which does not rely simply on the assertion that retribution is the only proper aim. Even a utilitarian can have misgivings about penalties which 'treat offenders as means' to benefit others, *if those penalties do them harm*. One might try to reassure him by pointing out that offenders have shown no such regard for their victims; but that would be rhetoric of a retributive kind. His misgivings need to be discussed without invoking desert.

The first point to be made is that we see nothing wrong in inflicting pain or distress when it is clearly in the interests of the person on whom it is inflicted, as surgery and dentistry are. If the person is a sane adult of normal or above normal intelligence we prefer to do so with his or her consent; but we forgo this preference in the case of children and the mentally ill or impaired. We usually allow the normal adult but not the others to decide what is in their best interests, even if we know better. Yet we do not apply this principle when we inflict pain or distress on offenders. We inflict the discomforts of withdrawal on heroin-abusers, and the distress of imprisonment on other offenders, without seeking their consent, and in most cases without asking ourselves whether what we are doing is in their best interests. We may do what we can to ease the pains of drug withdrawal or the distress of incarceration; but we do not allow the offender's objections to prevail.

Non-offenders too are knowingly harmed for the benefit of others. Urban redevelopment evicts families from homes. Airports sacrifice the peace of a few for the convenience of many. Sufferers from some communicable diseases undergo irksome restrictions in the interests of public health. Soldiers are enlisted—not always voluntarily—to risk life and limb for country. The list of examples could be much longer. The short point is that anyone who condemns deterrent or precautionary sentences on the ground that they harm offenders for the sake of others must either condemn many of the things that are done to the innocent, or explain why only the guilty should be immune from being 'treated as means'.

Our objector's position, however, may be less extreme. After all, there are harms and harms. They range from mere inconvenience to agony or terror. They may be temporary, leaving the subject undamaged, or they may cripple him physically or psychologically for the greater part of his life. Lines can be drawn. Even with a person's consent we normally consider it wrong to do something to him that will cause his death, maim him, or disfigure him, although we are prepared to risk this in the case of consenting—or even unconsenting—servicemen. Even in the case of offenders penal codes distinguish the harms which it is permissible to inflict and those which it is not. Most jurisdictions prohibit maiming, castration, disfigurement, and torture, and an increasing number no longer allow capital punishment. (As we shall see in Chapter 16 the underlying principle seems to be neither retributive nor utilitarian but humanitarian.) Our objector could reasonably follow suit and ask that sentences which are imposed for the benefit of others should not involve certain sorts of harm. He might define them as harms which damage people's bodies or minds; and he might add harms which make it very difficult for them to enjoy a tolerable and lawful way of life after the penal system has finished with them.

For our present purpose it hardly matters exactly where he draws the line. The point is that this sort of objector can object to some but not all deterrents or precautionary sentences. He can rule out capital punishment, castration, the amputation of hands, and other maimings, but hardly fines, community service, and other forms of compulsory attendance for work or training. Custodial sentences may give him trouble; and he will have to make distinctions. Most prisoners, as we saw in Chapter 4, survive them without lasting deterioration; but some are psychologically vulnerable. Very long sentences affect the 'quality of life' for a quite substantial fraction of it, and he might want to stipulate a maximum duration. This position, however, is not an objection to deterrent or precautionary sentences *as such*.

ii. Mistakes

But when precautionary sentences are under discussion it is another sort of objection that is more often put forward. More precisely, it is put forward when the sentence takes the form of elimination or long incarceration. It is hardly ever heard when all that is under consideration is disqualification from driving (or some other dangerous activity) or a ban on resorting to certain places (an example being the French *interdiction de séjour*). The reasoning must be that these entail a minimum of interference with liberty.

iii. Erroneous execution

The objection in question is based on the possibility of a mistake. It was first raised as an argument against capital punishment. Notoriously it sometimes turns out that a person who has been executed was not the person who committed the capital crime, or—more rarely—that he had committed it in a state of mind or in circumstances that should have excused him.

Although still urged by opponents of the death penalty it is not in strict logic an argument against *any* use of the death penalty, because it carries the clear implication that if not mistaken the death penalty would have been acceptable. All it demonstrates is that police, courts, prosecutors, and defence lawyers should take more care. It is worth noting that in the last few decades in which Britain used the death penalty, the civil servants who advised ministers whether it should be commuted to imprisonment applied a test called 'the scintilla of doubt'. Even though juries were instructed not to convict of murder if there was '*reasonable* doubt' about the guilt of the accused, there were cases in which some feature of the case against him raised a 'scintilla'—a tiny spark—of doubt, which was regarded, in spite of the verdict of a unanimous jury, as sufficient to justify the decision that the mandatory death penalty should not be inflicted. This preserved the lives of some accused who may have been innocent; but in spite of this practice there were one or two cases in which evidence was later unearthed to suggest that an innocent person had been executed.

That did not mean—as is often assumed by objectors—that a mistake was possible in every capital case. In practice many murderers admitted their guilt; and others were convicted on evidence which left no doubt about it. If what is at issue is the question whether capital punishment should *ever* be used, the argument from mistakes is not merely irrelevant: it implies, as has been pointed out, that in some cases it is justified. There are powerful arguments against the death penalty, but this is not one of them.

iv. Mistakes about the future

Paradoxically, mistakes seem—at first sight anyway—to be a sounder basis for objection when they are mistakes not about guilt but about the likelihood that a person will commit a crime in the future. Every jurisdiction has laws which allow persons convicted of very serious crimes to be detained for longer than ordinary sentencing practice would allow if there seems to be a substantial risk that their release would lead to their committing other serious crimes. These laws are usually confined to lists of specified crimes, and some countries' lists are longer than others. The procedures leading to such sentences differ, as do the procedures for deciding when it is reasonably safe to release the prisoner, and what conditions he should be required to observe after release. The differences are relevant only in so far as this or that procedure seems—to the prisoner or to lawyers—to lead to fairer decisions about the likelihood of mistakes.

The mistakes that worry anti-protectionists are about prisoners' futures, not their pasts. They emphasize the fact that many people who have served sentences for serious crimes such as homicide, rape, or other bodily harm do not repeat them. They concede—if they are realistic—that some less harmful sorts of offender do tend to repeat themselves: thieves, conmen, indecent exposers. But they maintain that it is a *minority* of murderers, rapists, and robbers who do so. If so, a policy which detains them for longer than a normal sentence would make more mistakes about their futures than would a policy which releases them. If only one in every three[2] men convicted of serious violence is likely to commit further violence after release, then releasing them all would involve only one mistake, while detaining them all would involve two.

One could quarrel about the statistics on which this argument is based. Some researchers have failed to realize that a follow-up which is meant to answer the question 'Do they ever again . . . ?' needs to be longer than one which is merely an attempt to compare the corrective efficacy of different types of sentence. The latter needs to cover only the first two or three years of liberty: the former needs to cover five or six years at least.[3] (About sexual offenders one cannot be quite so categorical. Many sexual offences are not reported, especially if the victims are children; and this makes the statistics unreliable.) Again, it is possible to define *subgroups* of violent offenders in such a way that the probability that a member of the subgroup will commit further violence is much greater than one third. In three British samples which I studied adult men with four or more convictions for violence were found to have probabilities well over 60 per cent, and in the best sample over 80 per cent.[4]

v. The arithmetical fallacy

It is possible, however, to grant that a majority of serious offenders will not commit further serious offences and yet to point to a crucial fallacy in the anti-protectionist case. The fallacy lies in counting mistakes of two kinds without acknowledging the all-important difference between them. The mistakes involved in detaining prisoners who, if one could only know their futures, would be non-repeaters are regrettable because they entail unnecessary deprivation of liberty and the other hardships of incarceration. But the mistakes involved in releasing a repeater mean that at least one more person—or occasionally the same person—will become the victim of a damaging crime. To lump the two kinds of mistake together and simply adopt a policy that will minimize their number is to fall for what I call 'the arithmetical fallacy'.

The arithmetical fallacy involves not one but two furtive assumptions. The second is that mistakes which turn out to have imposed unnecessary and unpleasant restraints are not merely regrettable but morally wrong. Hence the anti-protectionists' assertion that we have a duty to minimize their number. Certainly such a mistaken choice would be morally wrong if

1. its maker could be expected to know or ascertain enough to avoid it; and
2. there was an alternative which was clearly less likely to harm anyone.

But in the situation under discussion neither of these conditions is fulfilled. No matter how much care the deciders take to collect information about the offender's past, his conduct in prison (or in a mental hospital), his response to tests and interviews, and the social relationships to which he would return if released, they cannot *know* his future. They cannot be sure that release would not end in grave harm to someone else. When both choices involve the possibility of damaging mistakes one cannot label one of the choices as morally inexcusable simply on the basis of arithmetic. One can do so only by assigning different moral values to the different results of different sorts of mistake. This means that an anti-protectionist who resorts to the arithmetical argument but denies that he is equating the results of the two kinds of mistake must be implying something quite startling: that a policy which adds to the number of victims is morally better than one which merely adds to the length of a sentence.

vi. Punishing in advance

Protectionists have sounder arguments. The victims of mistaken releases are usually innocent victims (although a few contribute to their victimization by provocative conduct). The victims of mistaken detentions are not innocent: they have been found guilty of the sort of offence against which the detainers are trying to protect innocent victims. But an official committee in Sweden have offered an answer to this:

The ethical problem is that incapacitation as a reason for penal intervention means that a person is punished not for what he has done but for what it is believed he may do in the future. A person exposed to a sanction that is more severe than that which the crime he committed usually entails, and justified by the fact that he is to be prevented from recidivating will thereby serve a sentence for a crime he did not commit and which in addition it is doubtful if he will ever commit. This conflicts with essential demands for legal security and can be compared to the sentencing of an innocent person.[5]

Their answer, however, begs at least two questions. Must the length of a period of detention be determined by retributive considerations, as they assume? We shall see in Part III that this is something which cannot be assumed: it must be argued. Again, even if that assumption is granted, may a sentence not have any aim in addition to retributive propriety? The Swedish committee would readily allow that general deterrence is a proper additional aim. Why do they not allow that public protection is? Their answer must be that retributive reasoning dictates not only the minimum but also the maximum length of incarceration that is acceptable, which implies that the normal sentence for his actual crime is exactly—or almost exactly—'right'.

Return, however, to the point that a prisoner who may be the 'victim' of a mistaken prolongation of his detention is not an innocent victim: it is a point which needs discussion in less crude terms than those employed by either protectionists or the Swedish committee. In Britain the Floud Committee[6] were subtler. Essentially their argument was this. Members of the public have to put up with the risk of being victimized by people who have not yet been found guilty of victimizing. With exceptions—such as mentally disordered people who threaten violence—the unconvicted are allowed to benefit from a presumption of harmlessness. It would be impracticable to attempt to adopt any other policy.[7] When a person is found guilty of a harmful offence, however, he forfeits the presumption of harmlessness. This makes it permissible for the criminal justice system to dispose of him on the assumption that he presents a risk of future harm of a similar kind. Not that it makes it obligatory to do so: it merely gives a court the right to consider whether a precautionary sentence is called for.

Not everyone is prepared to talk in the language of 'rights'. The Floud Committee's argument, however, can be put in 'right-free' terms. For reasons which are practical, systems have to treat unconvicted people as harmless.[8] Most convicted people, too, are sentenced on the assumption that the sentence will deter or otherwise dissuade them from reoffending. But our law allows courts to impose special sentences on a selection of convicted people, the selection being determined by apprehension as to what they may do in the future. So much is fact. At this point the Floud Committee were entitled to ask 'What is wrong with that?' and place the burden of proof on those who say that it is wrong. The latter cannot rest their objection on a right not to be detained for society's protection, or any other right, if the language of rights has been ruled out. It seems that, like the Swedish committee, they must resort to invoking retributive principles. Once again retribution rears its head, and we have almost reached the stage at which the discussion of it need be postponed no longer.

7

The Sacrosanct Personality

WE must first, however, consider C. S. Lewis's objection to one utilitarian aim. Like Kant, he thought that offenders should be penalized because they deserve it. Like Kant, he did not mind if penalizing them had useful by-products such as general deterrence. But his objection is distinguishable from Kant's.

His article was called 'The Humanitarian Theory of Punishment'. He chose the adjective 'humanitarian' in preference to 'utilitarian' because 'those who hold it think that it is mild and merciful . . . I believe that the "Humanity" which it claims is a dangerous illusion and disguises the possibility of cruelty and injustice without end'.[1] Injustice is possible because 'humanitarians' might want to detain offenders for treatment (or general deterrence or the protection of society) for longer periods than they deserve. They might even want to penalize innocent people in the interests of general deterrence, since the public could thus be induced to believe that law-breaking leads to punishment oftener than in fact it does.

i. Human dignity

These are important points, which receive the consideration they deserve in Chapters 6 and 11. Here, however, we are concerned with Lewis's central objection. Although he does not actually use the phrase 'human dignity', this is the core of what he is saying, for example in his purple passage:

To be 'cured' against one's will and cured of states which we may not regard as disease is to be put on a level with those who have not yet reached the age of reason or those who never will: to be classed with infants, imbeciles, and domestic animals. But to be punished, however severely, because we have deserved it, because we 'ought to have known better', is to be treated as a human person made in God's image.

At first sight this looks like nothing more than a vague and more rhetorical restatement of Kant's objection, invoking human rationality, the supremacy of retribution, and—though Kant made less of it—God. That would be a superficial interpretation. The passage would make sense without the praise of retribution and without the reference to God.

ii. Children, imbeciles, and animals

What is unacceptable for Lewis is the way in which attempts to 'cure' offenders of offending appear to demote them to a status which we usually reserve for children, imbeciles,[2] and animals. As he points out, earlier cultures would have added slaves to his catalogue. But the example which makes his point really clear is 'animals'. Trying to 'cure' offenders, whether it succeeds or not, amounts to denying them the status of human beings.

Interestingly, it is clear from the rest of his article that what he found most objectionable was 'cures' by psychotherapy. This is interesting not only because he overestimated the extent to which psychotherapeutic techniques were actually being employed at the time; nor because he pictures them as being applied by 'men in white coats'. What is more important, and paradoxical, is that these techniques, whether successful or not, are *less* open than any other to the accusation that they ignore what is special about human beings. They have aptly been called 'the talking cure', and—with eccentric exceptions—their aim is to make their subjects more aware of the irrational determinants of their feelings and conduct, and if possible more able to bring them within the control of their rationality.

That is not to assert that psychotherapy is an *effective* tool for dealing with delinquency. It merely raises the question why Lewis considers it an *objectionable* tool. He does not, for example, explicitly object to individual deterrence, possibly because that clearly assumes rationality in the offender. It is probably safe to assume that he would have objected to the techniques called 'behaviour modification', which rely on positive or negative conditioning. Unlike psychotherapy this works with animals, and would thus have been a better target for the blunderbuss which he is firing. But in his day the application of behaviour modification to sinners had barely begun to be talked about.³ It is a fair assumption, too, that he would have objected on similar grounds to the castration of sex offenders, or the use of drugs to diminish sexual or violent urges.

iii. Lack of consent

Both in the passage quoted and elsewhere, he emphasizes the non-voluntary nature of what he is objecting to. Lack of consent is more important than lack of success. (Yet 'talking cures' cannot work without the patient's consent!) This is consistent with the way in which he differentiates between sane adults and certain other categories. We do not seek the consent of animals to what we inflict on them by way of training or treatment. It is often uncertain whether an 'imbecile's' consent is based on sufficient understanding to be genuine. As for children, if they withhold consent to what we think will do them good, we are apt to override them.

Lack of consent, however, cannot be the essence of what he dislikes. If it were, he would object to the infliction of deserved punishment unless the offender willingly accepted it. Another passage makes what he dislikes a little clearer:

To be taken without consent from my home and friends: to lose my liberty; to undergo all those assaults on my personality which modern psychotherapy knows how to deliver; to be remade after some pattern of 'normality' hatched in a Viennese laboratory to which I never professed allegiance . . . Only enormous ill-desert could justify it; but ill-desert is the very conception which the Humanitarian theory has overthrown.

It would be unfair to dismiss his point by ridiculing his fears of 'Viennese laboratories',⁴ or his belief that psychotherapy could obliterate what was special about his personality. His point is that his personality is sacrosanct. Other, less well-known, writers have adopted a similar standpoint: for example Nicholas Kittrie in his book *The Right to be Different*.⁵ Like Lewis they seem prepared to admit exceptions. His exception was cases of 'enormous ill-desert'. Writers such as Kittrie are not interested in desert, but make exceptions for personalities which lead their owners to do grave harm to others.

More important, however, is the way in which Lewis made

an exception of children. It is reminiscent of John Stuart Mill's view that it was justifiable to coerce children and 'barbarians' into acting in their own best interests, but not adults, or at least not English adults.[6] Nowadays some writers in the United States would even question whether parents should attempt to mould their children's personalities.[7] That certainly has one merit: it side-steps the difficulty of drawing a line between childhood and adulthood. Lewis does not tell us at which birthday a personality becomes sacrosanct, or whether a particularly childish personality—of the kind owned by many adult offenders—is non-sacrosanct. Nor, of course, how imbecile one has to be distinguishable from a sane adult.

iv. The right of ownership

These are debating-points, however. Essentially what Lewis did was to declare a right; and it is not easy to argue with someone who does that. It is the tactic of a person who values something so much that he wants to make it unassailable. People have ascribed rights to animals and even inanimate landscapes, ignoring Hart's point that the owner of a right must be capable of choosing whether to claim it or not. It is arguable that there are a few rights which should never be disclaimed, the right to life being an example. But Lewis is not taking up this position. He concedes that, like other rights of ownership, this one allows the owner to consent to interference; and he even grants exceptions in which interference is justified without the owner's consent: the personalities of children, imbeciles, and people whose conduct is of 'enormous ill-desert'. In the case of children and imbeciles his reasoning must have been that they are not capable of making sensible choices, so that sane adults are justified in making sensible choices on their behalf. In cases of enormous ill-desert he may have reasoned that the ill-desert forfeits the right to choose. In both sorts of case the implication is that a sensible chooser would allow his personality to be improved. This makes it difficult to see why improvement is not justified in the case of a sane adult whose conduct, though not of enormous ill-desert, is nevertheless harmful to others.

The best that can be done when someone asserts a disclaimable right is to ask him whether it is conditional. Does a person (or animal, or waterfall) have the right even when the exercise of it interferes with the exercise of the same (or other) right by someone or something else? If not, is the right forfeited, or is the exercise of it restricted to what will not interfere with others' rights? Lewis and Kittrie seem prepared to make concessions of this sort. Lewis concedes cases of 'enormous ill-desert': Kittrie concedes serious harm to others. Unlike Kant's and Duff's right to be treated as autonomous beings (see Chapter 9), Lewis's and Kittrie's rights are conditional. This means that they are, in theory at least, negotiable, in the sense that we can expect Lewis or Kittrie to be prepared to discuss where to draw the line beyond which the right should not be exercised and cannot be claimed as a bar to 'assaults on personality'. They should, for example, be prepared to consider making exceptions of cases in which an alteration of the personality—supposing this to be achievable—would not only make life safer for other people but also make it pleasanter for the owner of the personality. And so on.

PART III
Retributivism

WHATEVER one thinks of the moral objections discussed in Part II, there is no doubt that a utilitarian approach to penalizing people suffers from one discouraging feature. As we saw in Part I it is seldom possible for a sentencer—or other penalizer—to be sure in a given case that the choice he has in mind will have any effect on the future volume of crime or other infringements. The only exceptions are measures which eliminate the offender or incapacitate him; and these are not always permissible or tolerable.

The retributive approach is an encouraging contrast. It promises the certainty which utilitarianism cannot. The punisher can be sure that whatever else he may or may not be achieving he is at least inflicting more or less what the offender deserves. If he is a thoroughgoing retributivist—and not one of the compromising kinds discussed in Chapter 15—he regards it as his duty to do so: he is under a moral obligation to inflict deserts.

The notion of desert involves the notion of blaming; and this is the subject of Chapter 8. The belief that the infliction of desert is in some way obligatory seems to need an explanation; and Chapter 9 discusses the attempts of retributivists to offer satisfactory explanations. Since they all suffer from serious defects, Chapter 10 considers a possible improvement which has not, to my knowledge at least, been suggested by retributivists, although at least one was once on the verge of doing so.

There is also, however, a 'negative principle' which is regarded as an important and valuable part of retributivism. Hart called it 'retribution in distribution'. Roughly stated, the principle is that the innocent should never be penalized. Chapter 11 discusses the two kinds of 'innocence', and whether the principle is necessarily retributive.

Chapter 12 discusses *what* is deserved, and how it is possible to be sure that penalties accurately inflict it, and are not too severe or too lenient.

Chapters 13 and 14 deal with aspects of retributive punishment which are often ignored. 'Vicarious' punishment is sometimes discussed, but can be confused with what, for want of a better name, I have called '*obiter*' punishment. There are also 'natural' and 'incidental' varieties to be considered. Finally, forgiveness and mercy, which most philosophers prefer to leave to theologians, are the main subjects of Chapter 14, together with remorse, repentance, and reparation.

8

Blaming and Excusing

THE original meaning of retribution was 'paying back' a literal debt or tax. Later it came to mean rewarding a good act with a benefit or a bad one with harm. Some philosophers still argue that the notion of repayment explains its appeal.[1] Etymology, however, is not always the best of guides to current meanings, especially when they have been refined or distorted by much discussion. In the philosophy of punishment there is no doubt that the retributive justification for a penalty is linked to what a person has done, not what he will do. One may promise punishment (or reward) for a future action, but to award it in advance would somehow seem to make it something else: a deterrent or incentive. The 're' in 'reward', 'repayment', and 'retribution' points to the past, and suggests that it must be *re*flected in what is being done now. There must be some sort of equivalence.

The notion of equivalence is of course most evident in what are called 'talionic'[2] punishments, which inflict on the offender what he has inflicted on his victim. Although they were commoner in early penal codes than they are nowadays, the death penalty for homicide survives as a modern example. Yet even when the penalty is not of the talionic kind the need for equivalence of some sort is still felt. The gravity of the harm done is still regarded as something that should determine the severity of the penalty (or at least limit it: see Chapter 15).

i. Blaming

Harm done, however, is modified by intention in the eyes of modern retributivists. An accidental killing is not punished as if it were murder. An attempted murder, even if it does no actual harm, is punished almost as severely as a successful one. If we were strictly logical the punishment would be equally severe: incompetence does not mitigate. Other things do mitigate—or aggravate—the blame. A poor woman who steals to feed her children is blamed less than one who embezzles in order to support her ostentatious life-style. Other 'mitigators' are provocation, intentional temptation by a victim, youth or old age, mental disorder, the 'staleness' of an offence committed long ago, and evidence of good character. The last two are especially interesting, for a reason which will be explained in a moment.

ii. Excusing

There are factors which do more than mitigate, and persuade us to reduce blame to zero. Examples are the states known to lawyers as 'automatism', in which the bodily movements that caused harm are not willed by the body's owner (as happens in sneezes, epileptic fits, and sleep-walking); violence in self-defence (provided that it is not excessive and that escape is out of the question); necessity (jettisoning a cargo, for instance, in order to save a ship); mental disorders of a kind that prevents a person from realizing what he is doing, or that it is illegal (or, in some jurisdictions, from resisting a desire or impulse); honest mistake (as when one appropriates the wrong umbrella).

Obviously there are also aggravating considerations: premeditation, professionalism, abuse of positions of authority or trust; sadism and unnecessary violence; harm done to someone to whom the offender owed gratitude; the helpless or pitiable state of the victim; and—again of special interest—previous offending, particularly of the same kind.

iii. Character

Previous offending, good character, and the 'staleness' of the offence are of special interest because they are controversial: retributivists split over their relevance. The great majority hold that we should blame and punish only for 'actions[3] plus states of mind'. On this view good character does not mitigate and previous offending does not aggravate. (The offenders with whom I used to discuss the point are also of this view; but since most of them had poor records they were not impartial.) A few philosophers,[4] however, see that evidence of good or bad behaviour is relevant after all if what is being blamed is *moral character*. On this view the offender is blamed for being a person of the sort which is normally capable of doing whatever he did. It does not go as far as blaming him for being the sort of person who merely thinks of killing, raping, or thieving: an action is required to satisfy us that he is the sort of person who translates thoughts into deeds. Previous good behaviour, on the other hand, undermines this inference, and makes us wonder whether the act was perhaps 'out of character'. When the offence occurred many years ago we wonder whether the offender is still capable of it. Conversely, repeated offending of the same kind not only confirms that he is *capable* of turning thought into action but suggests that he is *likely* to. This view not only makes sense of taking character evidence into account: it also fits the other mitigating, excusing, and aggravating factors which courts take into account. Mitigations and excuses tell us that what the actor did should not be regarded as an indication that he is *normally* capable of it, because the circumstances were exceptional, or at least such that most people would have done likewise. Aggravations tell us that his moral character is even worse than the act itself suggests.

Perhaps it is no more than an intriguing fact that, while most penal codes and sentencing practices allow character factors to be taken into account, most retributive sentencers believe that they are supposed to be punishing offenders for 'actions plus states of mind' and not for moral character. It is only academic theorists who point out that whatever courts think they are doing they may really be doing something with different implications.

9

Justifying Retribution

IN Christian, Judaic, and Islamic cultures there are many people to whom the retributive justification seems to need no further explanation. It has scriptural authority. It is reinforced by dislike of those who flout accepted rules, and by sympathy for the victims of their conduct. To question it, seems like questioning the obligation to keep a promise, the very definition of which includes the obligation.

Even utilitarians seem to agree that the commission of an offence is needed to justify a penalty (although their reasoning needs the thorough discussion which it will receive in Chapter 11). Yet the mere existence of utilitarians, and their feeling that some future benefit is required to complete the justification, should convince even the most devout retributivist that his justification calls for explanation and examination; and in fact most retributive philosophers have seen the need to offer explanations.

A few 'intuitionists' see a trap here, and step round it by arguing that the duty to punish is something which we simply 'intuit'; that is, perceive rather than infer by reasoning. This is not an easy position, because there is an awkward fact which does have to be explained: the fact that by no means everyone perceives retribution as a duty. It is true that other kinds of perception are lacking in a few people: the blind or the stone-deaf, for example. In such cases, however, the defect is explainable. An inability to perceive the need to punish can be plausibly explained as the effect of certain kinds of upbringing; but this explanation does not suit the intuitionist, since it suggests that the perception which he posits is really a learned reaction to offending rather than an inborn intuition. Intuitionists are not extinct,[1] but very rare, at least where retribution is concerned.

i. Debts to society

Non-intuitionists' explanations range from the simple to the complex, from the metaphorical to the literal, from the super-stitious to the practical. The simplest, as we have seen, relies on the etymology of the word. Retribution is paying what is owed. Prisoners are 'paying a debt to society'. Taken literally this seems to confuse society with the victim. We do regard offenders as owing their victims restitution or compensation, especially if the court has made an order to this effect (see Chapter 14). But the very fact that we distinguish restitution from punishment emphasizes the fact that the latter is some-thing quite different from a literal debt. (Admittedly society has incurred expenses in bringing the offender to justice; but we call that 'costs'.) If society is being compensated for anything, it is for the breach of its peace.[2] It is true that members of a society may feel more at peace when a murderer, robber, or rapist is eliminated or locked up for what they believe to be a long time. But the analogy of a debt breaks down completely when we reflect that unsuccessful attempts and plans to commit offences are regarded as deserving punishment. If I try to raise a loan and fail I do *not* owe a debt to anyone, but if I try to commit a crime apparently I do.

Metaphors may help us to understand an explanation, but to accept them *as* explanations is another matter. It would imply that we have no hope of formulating or being offered a literal explanation that we can understand. We are sometimes in this position: for example when a computer scientist is trying to explain the operation of a complex program. We allow him to say that the computer 'compares', 'rejects', or even, when it plays chess, 'lays traps', because a literal description of its activities would be unintelligible to us. Religious exponents of retributivism might claim that we cannot really understand God's reason for wanting sinners punished, and must be content with a metaphor or metaphors. That does not mean, however, that we are obliged to accept a metaphor that seems inadequate, and particularly one that is as deficient as the 'debt to society'.

ii. Annulment

The most obviously metaphorical explanation is that the penalty *annuls* the crime. When the criminal has been punished it is as if the crime had not been committed. As anyone who has been mugged or raped is aware, this is nonsense. Victims can be compensated, but not unraped or unmugged. Yet Hegel and more surprisingly the Edwardian philosopher Bosanquet seem to offer this explanation. It is true that later in the same chapter Bosanquet seems to be talking about the function of punishment in conveying a message:

Some overt act is also necessary . . . to make sure that the dullest capacity, including that of the guilty person . . . shall not fail to apprehend the intensity of the annulling act.[3]

It is less nonsensical to claim that public punishment—or more precisely the public promise of punishment—is a ritual act which helps people to feel that the crime has not taken place. The trouble is that it just is not true. Even the dullest capacity must be aware that 'dead men rise up never', even when you hang their murderers. Sentencing may have a ritual function, but whatever the ritual celebrates it is not annulment.

It has been argued[4] that Hegel meant something more subtle and tenable: that a crime is a denial of a victim's right—whether to life, to property, or something else—and that punishment is a public declaration that the denial of such a right was mistaken. Punishment is a reassertion of the victim's right. This reduces the notion of annulment to a rather special version of denunciation (see Chapter 3), and does not explain why the reassertion of a right need take the form of a sentence; or, if a sentence is the only kind of reassertion that is sufficiently emphatic, why it needs actually to be carried out. Again, suppose that the crime is a murder which has never been recognized as such, so that the denial of the victim's right to life has never been heard, is there, on this theory, any need to reassert it?

iii. Rectifying unfair advantage

There is a less metaphorical version of the 'annulment' explanation: that a law-breaker has taken an unfair advantage which can be taken away from him by a penalty. He has usurped property, pleasure, or power in a way that is not open to the law-abiding man, who either has to go without or work harder for the same desiderandum. Penalties put matters right, either by removing what the offender has gained or by imposing a disadvantage, as do penalties in games.[5]

It is not quite so easy to say what is wrong with this explanation. It relies on an analogy rather than a metaphor, since it can be phrased without mentioning games; but it could hardly occur to someone who was unfamiliar with the rules of football, cricket, or baseball. That does not discredit it: a good analogy can be illuminating. As in games, we feel that the penalty should in some way reflect the seriousness of the infringement. If the foul prevented a certain goal, a goal should be awarded. If a player endangers others, he should be sent off. If a drug-dealer makes a lot of money, he should forfeit it. And many people believe that he who takes a life should forfeit his own, or at least be excluded from the community.

Nor is it an objection to point out that there are many ways of 'taking advantage' for which we do not feel that people should be punished. A man or woman may succeed in commerce because they have sources of capital, or useful acquaintances, which other people do not have; yet even egalitarians do not think they should be punished. Games, too, are not without analogous inequalities. A tall high-jumper is likely to beat a short one. British skiers are disadvantaged by lack of home-grown snow. Some sports try to compensate for natural inequalities. Boxers are subdivided according to body-weight. Fencers must use foils of equal length (but their reach is not included in the measurement). There are separate competitions for immature and elderly tennis-players.

What is penalized in games, and sometimes by the law, is the *deliberate* taking of an advantage forbidden by the rules. To regard all law-breaking, however, as moves in a competitive game is unrealistic. A man who assaults another is not really competing with him. Not all crime is instrumental, committed with the intention of securing some benefit. Some of it—and especially unplanned violence—is expressive, giving vent to emotion. Again, when a man forces his sexual attentions on someone, it is a distortion to describe him as taking advantage of men who proceed by persuasion. If he and his victim were alone on an island there would be no competition but still a wrong which retributivists would want to punish. Attempts, too, raise an awkward question, as they did when the debt metaphor was offered. Should an unsuccessful effort to commit a crime, which has brought no advantage to anyone, be penalized by the imposition of a disadvantage? Most retributivists would feel obliged to say 'Yes'. Duff makes another good point:[6]

What kind of attitude is expressed in the thought that the immoral or criminal agent has gained an unfair profit? That thought is most familiar when we ourselves are tempted by the wrongdoer's actions: we think that someone who has profited by trickery or deceit could do so only because others restrain themselves from such immoral methods— and that we could do as well as him if we did not thus restrain ourselves; we watch a dishonest entrepreneur, or a colleague on the fiddle, or an adulterous spouse, with envious and self-righteously disapproving eyes. Surely, however, we do not think of the murderer or rapist in such terms as these or, if our condemnation of them does reflect such thoughts, we should surely feel ashamed of ourselves for being thus tempted by what they do. This suggests that the idea that the wicked profit unfairly by their wrong-doing reflects a grudging and less than whole-hearted commitment to the values which they flout . . .

It is a moralistic rather than a logical point; but none the less sharp for that.

iv. A metaphysical justification

Kant himself resorted not to metaphors but to metaphysics.[7] The duty to punish was a 'categorical imperative'. Many imperatives were 'hypothetical', their force depending on their practical consequences. Categorical imperatives were of the moral kind which do not depend on consequences. Man, though existing in the visible world of nature, must also recognize himself as 'pure intelligence in an existence not dependent on the condition of time'. As such he must recognize not only practical imperatives but categorical ones as well. An important categorical imperative is 'So act as to treat humanity, whether in thine own person or that of any other, in every case as an end withal, never as means only': a dictum which was discussed in Chapter 6. And one of its corollaries seems to be the categorical imperative to follow this doctrine by punishing offenders as they deserve. Man's rational, autonomous nature exists as an end in itself: it is why he must always be treated as an end; that is, in ways that acknowledge his capacity for acting in accordance with reason.

Kant's own views as to what offenders deserved were simple and talionic: a death for a death, a dishonourable fate for a dishonourable act, and so on. But that is by the way. More to the point is his reason for believing that inflicting desert was the only way of treating an offender as an end. His attempt to be explicit about it was his famous dictum about 'the last murderer':

Even if a civil society were to dissolve itself by common agreement . . . the last murderer remaining in prison must first be executed so that . . . the blood-guilt thereof will not be fixed on the people . . .[8]

Yet this fails to answer two awkward questions. First, is it not too imprecise to say that those who failed to execute him would share *his* guilt? They might very well be guilty of something, but it would hardly be murder. In Kant's own terms it would be more accurate to call them guilty of omission to obey a categorical imperative. But this does not explain the categorical imperative. For it is not clear why they ought to deal with the last murderer in a *punitive* way. Why would they not escape guilt if they simply succeeded in persuading him to repent, and renounce homicide?[9] Why is making an end of a murderer the only way in which he can be treated as an end? Kant was an early believer in a social contract of sorts. Autonomous, noumenal man is a member (willy-nilly) of a society which must recognize the categorical imperative that dictates the punishment of crimes. Why it dictates retributive punishment rather than utilitarian correction he does not explain.

v. Spiritual improvement

Some Christian theologians,[10] however, see the justification for retributive punishment in the repentance or other spiritual improvement which it may induce in the sinner. To equate this with 'reform' of a secular kind, and thus dismiss them as theological utilitarians would perhaps be too crude. After all, it is not long ago that a bishop of Durham, speaking in a convocation, justified a particular execution on the grounds that the condemned man underwent 'the most wonderful reclamation and conversion that I have ever seen'.[11] A utilitarian would not regard a dead man's conversion as benefiting society. Admittedly when murderers or other offenders serve long sentences they sometimes express repentance; but it is not easy to be sure whether the repentance is genuine or professed in the hope of parole. When it is genuine—as it sometimes is—it is likely to be the result not of incarceration but of the ministrations of chaplains or probation officers.

The question which these theologians must be prepared to answer is 'How do you then justify punishment in cases in which the offender persists in maintaining that his action was morally right (as some politically motivated offenders do, to cite only one sort of example)?' There are offenders who are most unlikely to be brought to repentance by any punishment that can be inflicted on them. Is the idea of punishing them to be abandoned, or justified by the feeble reply that one can never be certain that it will not help them to see the error of their ways?

vi. Retribution as communication

It is not only theologians, however, who see retribution as an attempt to communicate with the offender: many 'modern retributivists' do so. Modernity is relative. The Victorian philosopher Bradley[12] hinted at this view when he wrote that 'Punishment is the denial of wrong by the assertion of right'; but he did not pursue the point. Von Hirsch does:

The account of desert offered in this book does not pre-suppose arcane notions of 'righting' the moral imbalance wrought by criminal misconduct. In *Doing Justice* I did at one point speak of punishment as restoring a correct allocation of the 'benefits' and 'burdens' of wrongdoing. I am now convinced such explanations are unenlightening. Desert in punishment can rest on a much simpler idea, used in everyday discourse: the idea of censure ... Punishment connotes censure. Penalties should comport with the seriousness of crimes, so that the reprobation visited on the offender through his penalty fairly reflects the blameworthiness of his conduct.[13]

Duff, too, offers 'an ideal account of criminal punishment as a communicative enterprise in which we engage with the criminal'. He sees punishment as an enforced penance through which the criminal can 'strengthen and express her repentant understanding and restore herself to the community from which her crime threatened to separate her: the proper purpose of punishment'.[14]

Although Duff is much influenced by Kant, and von Hirsch makes it plain that he was originally a Kantian retributivist, it is clear from these quotations what distinguishes 'just deserters' from the Kantian tradition. Their justification for inflicting desert is its beneficial effect on people. Von Hirsch sees the benefit (or the main benefit: he is not explicit) in the effect on the moral values of people other than the offender; and he admits that this makes him a utilitarian of sorts. Duff sees the benefit—or the main benefit—as the effect on the offender. In his eyes it is like the effect of penance on a member of the Roman Catholic Church. Especially striking is his remark that punishment enables the offender to be 'restored to the community'. The medieval Christian Fathers declared that penances restored the penitent to the communion of the Church.

It seems relevant to point out that penance had to be preceded by confession and contrition, and must be undertaken voluntarily, or at least in obedience to the instruction of the confessor. Duff does not squarely face the fact that many offenders never admit their guilt, and that many who do are unrepentant; or that they do not enter prisons voluntarily or with uncoerced obedience. He could argue, perhaps, that such penalties as incarceration may be imposed *in the hope* that even an unrepentant and unwilling prisoner may 'get the message' during the course of his sentence, and undergo the moral change that will reconcile him to the community. His position would then be on all fours with that of the straightforward utilitarian who imprisons *in the hope* of deterring the offender, while admitting that his hope may not be fulfilled. The only difference would be that the utilitarian's hope is based on sounder empirical evidence.

However that may be, Duff turns out to be just another denouncer of a special sort (see Chapter 3). He is relying not so

much on the expressive effect which sentences are supposed to
have on the public as on the effect they are supposed to have on
the offender himself: a very narrow version of the utilitarian
justification. There is nothing wrong with that, except perhaps
that it shows how little contact he has had with offenders. But if
he wants to deny that he is a utilitarian he must go one step
further. He must say that the beneficial effect for which he
hopes does not include secular reform: that it does not matter
whether as a result the offender ceases to offend. Or, more
precisely perhaps, that if as a result he does cease to reoffend,
that would be a desirable by-product of his spiritual improvement, and fairly good evidence that his spiritual improvement
was genuine; but it would not be essential.

vii. 'Only connect'[15]

There is at least one retributivist, however, who sees punishment as communication of a sort which cannot be regarded as
tainted by utility. Robert Nozick writes that

The wrongdoer has become disconnected from correct values, and
the purpose of punishment is to (re) connect him. It is not that this
connection is a desired further effect of punishment: the act of retributive punishment itself effects this connection . . . Retributive punishment is to give correct values as significant an effect in someone's life
as the magnitude of his flouting these correct values . . . although the
linking of the person with correct values . . . does not depend upon
some further effect as with the teleological[16] retributivist, it can fail to
occur, just as an ordinary act of communication can fail if the recipient
is deaf, or does not understand the language. The linkage we are
delineating corresponds to the recipient of a verbal message *understanding* the assertion; whereas the goal of the teleological retributivist
corresponds to the recipient's *accepting* what is said. It is not so very
difficult to get someone to understand that they are being punished
because others view what they did as wrong, and intend for them to
realize this is happening.

Connecting an offender to correct values, to use Nozick's
highly metaphorical phrase, means making him *understand* that
he is being penalized because others, whose values are 'correct',
view what he did as wrong. He need not *accept* their values.
Desirable as that would be, to insist on it would make the

explanation utilitarian, as Nozick himself points out. Retributive punishment is thus a message from people whose values are assumed to be correct (at least as regards the offence in question) to someone whose act or omission has shown that his values are by their standards incorrect. The message need not have any effect on his incorrect values: it does not have to have utility. What it must do is affect his life in a way that corresponds in 'magnitude' to the offence. This is a talionic requirement: Nozick literally and explicitly means 'a life for a life'. For some murders the death sentence is the only appropriate message, even when its utility is nil, and even if the killer himself regards the message as undeserved.

We might ask what point there is in such a message. Nozick insists that the point is not utility of any kind: he is a 'non-teleological retributivist'. The point lies simply in the conveyance of the message to the offender (not merely to an audience, as in the ritual theories discussed in Chapter 3). What he seems to have lost sight of is the baby in the bath-water: the element of obligation which is an integral part of retributivism. He says nothing that explains why such a message *must* be delivered.

Von Hirsch sees the baby, and tries to save it. The State, he says, is under an obligation to respond in some way to criminal law-breaking. For von Hirsch this obligation seems not to be a retributive but a utilitarian one. At the same time, the State should respond.

in a manner that testifies to the recognition that the conduct is wrong. To respond in a morally neutral fashion, to treat the conduct merely as a source of costs to the perpetrator, is objectionable because it fails to provide this recognition.

This point is *not* utilitarian, for he goes on:

Even if we failed to discover evidence confirming that the criminal sanction reinforces people's desire to be law-abiding . . . the sanction should still express blame as an embodiment of moral judgments about criminal conduct.

This has narrowed the plug-hole, but still leaves room for the vanishing baby. If the message which expresses blame need have no utility, where lies the moral necessity? It is not hard, of course, to find a *psychological* necessity. Our feelings about a crime may well make us want to convey such a message to the criminal or an audience, but that is not a moral necessity. That baby has disappeared.

10

A Rule-explanation?

THERE is one explanation of the obligation to punish which is not metaphorical, metaphysical, theological, superstitious, or crypto-utilitarian. It is not very exciting, and is bound to disappoint retributivists who regard their stance as more dignified than utilitarianism. But it deserves serious consideration.

What needs to be explained is not disapproval of law-breaking or rule-breaking (most people wish there were less of it), nor dislike of those who indulge in it (most of them are not very likeable), nor even satisfaction with their punishment. There are obvious psychological explanations of these emotions. We sympathize with victims, are worried about the possibility of becoming victims, and value a law-abiding society. What needs to be explained is retributivists' feeling that retaliation against law-breakers is not merely justified but obligatory. What is it that makes retaliation a duty?

i. The rule-making animal[1]

The answer, I suggest, is that man is a rule-making animal. Rules account for far more of his behaviour than do 'instincts' or physical laws. Not that he is exempt from these influences. He is inexorably subject to the laws of gravity. His body burns just as well as the carcass of any other animal. He is driven by hunger and curiosity as much as any other primate. He is also a social animal. Unlike other social animals, however, he *regulates* his interactions with his fellows, and also with his non-human environment. Regulation means using rules. Even intelligible speech depends on rules. Other animals can communicate alarm, anger, or sexual desire by sounds; but these are not speech. Babies can make sounds which alert their parents to fears, anger, or needs; but in order to speak they must learn the rules first of meaning and then of grammar. The capacity for following grammatical rules may even be innate, according to some linguists. However that may be, man is clearly an animal with a peculiar propensity for making, learning, and following rules.

When children have learnt a little speech they are able to learn rules of conduct. Without speech they can learn a few things in the same way as animals do: the avoidance of pain from sharp or hot objects, for example. But it is only through the understanding of speech, and later through answers to questions, that they learn the difference between 'mine' and 'thine', and the existence of a host of prohibitions and injunctions which could not be assimilated by a process of mere conditioning. At the same time they do more than learn what they are expected to do and not to do; they acquire the *notion* of a rule. This happens even in families which never use the word: it is enough to say 'people don't do that' (however plain it may be that some do).

The older the child grows, the more transactions he will be involved in which are impossible without rules. A promise, for instance, would be a mere prediction come true. Games without rules would not be games. Borrowing implies returning, or at least offering to return. Marriage has rules, and so does most cohabitation.

Some kinds of social behaviour are less obviously rule-governed. The sociologist Garfinkel demonstrated this to his students by telling them to behave at home as if they were staying with people they did not know well: for instance asking permission to do things like taking a bath. This made their parents extremely uneasy, and in some cases angry. Their offspring were acting according to the wrong set of rules.[2] What the technique of 'Garfinkeling' showed was that some situations are subject to rules so subtle that their existence is made manifest only when they are broken.

At the other extreme are rules which are codified: prohibitions and injunctions in writing, with subsidiary rules defining what are and are not infringements. Most games have codified rules: so do most professional associations, trade unions, clubs, armed services, bureaucracies. The most obvious example is of course the criminal law.

ii. Penalizing rules

Most, if not quite all, codified sets of rules include penalizing rules, which lay down what is to be done with people who infringe the prohibitions or injunctions. Often they are prescriptive; that is, they prescribe what must be done. As we have seen, prescriptive penalizing rules are commoner in Continental codes than in Anglo-American ones. Even so, there are examples in British sentencing law: the life sentence for murder; disqualification for certain driving offences, fixed penalties for some minor traffic offences. Some American states have adopted prescriptive rules for the sentencing of felonies. Otherwise the penalizing rules are merely permissive, saying what *may* be done to the law-breaker, and by implication what may not be done.

It is the existence of a penalizing rule, whether in a code, a tradition, or an accepted practice, which legitimizes hostility to the law-breaker and allows the retributivist to feel that punishing him is obligatory, no matter what the consequences. Not to penalize him for his infringement would itself be an infringement: an unpunished infringement means two infringements. Like the parents of Garfinkel's students, retributivists feel that something has gone wrong if the penalizing rule is not complied with.

iii. The hard core of logic

It is always important to distinguish a psychological explanation from a logical one: but this one is both. The strength of retributivists' hostility to law-breakers is easily accounted for as a natural reaction to behaviour that is harmful, threatening, disgusting, or frustrating; but without penalizing rules it lacks legitimation. Experiments by social psychologists[3] have shown that people who would feel guilty about expressing hostility to others can be induced to do so without this feeling if they are provided with a legitimizing excuse. Rules are a powerful mode of legitimation. Moreover, there is a hard little core of logic inside the psychological explanation. If there is a rule which prescribes a penalty, then to refrain from penalizing an identified rule-breaker is to add another breach of the rules.

It does not matter why the rule was adopted in the first place. It may have been enacted by legislators who had deterrence or some other utilitarian aim in mind. My Introduction, however, emphasized the difference between justifying 'punishment as an institution' and justifying particular instances of it. The reasoning which justified a sentencing code, or a provision of a sentencing code, in the minds of those who created it, is not necessarily the reasoning of the sentencer when he applies it to an offender; and if he applies it chiefly because he wants to follow the rule he is applying it retributively.

iv. Objections

Genuine retributivists will no doubt find this explanation quite unsatisfactory. It reduces what they regard as a moral feeling to mere psychology and logic. It has none of the dignity of the explanations which were considered in Chapter 9. Dissatisfaction, however, is of two kinds. One is merely emotional: the other is based on objections which are arguable.

One arguable objection is that many penalizing rules are not prescriptive but permissive, and merely allow a penalty (or choice of penalties)[4] without being mandatory. Most British sentencing law is of this sort. Consequently, the argument goes, it does not account for the genuine retributivist's feeling that law-breakers ought to be penalized.

The first point to be made about this important objection is that there are in fact retributivists to whom permissive rules seem to be exactly what is wanted, because they regard retribution as a limiting principle, not a duty. They compromise with utilitarians by allowing the latter to dictate the aims of punishment, so long as its severity does not exceed what is retributively appropriate. Permissive sentencing rules set limits to fines, imprisonment, and other measures, but allow sentencers to make choices within these limits and with whatever aim they think right. This compromise with utilitarianism deserves a thorough discussion, which it will get in Chapter 15.

What satisfies a 'limiting retributivist', however, will not satisfy a genuine one, who needs something that makes punishment a duty. Yet to some extent even the British system provides this. Permissive sentencing statutes are backed up by non-statutory rules. The Magistrates' Association provides its members with lists of recommended penalties. It adds the rider that these should be adjusted to meet the circumstances of cases; but that—as we shall see in Chapter 12—need not be inconsistent with a retributive approach to punishment. For common offences each bench adopts its tariff, sometimes departing from the recommendations of the Association. Judges too have tariffs[5] in mind; and the Court of Appeal tries to promote consistency. Their respect for consistency means that in spite of the permissive nature of the statute they are obeying a mandatory rule.

By the same token a parent who penalizes a child, although he is following no printed code and no consensus with other parents, can be said to be acting retributively if his main reason is not the training of the child but some moral rule. He may have inherited the rule from his own upbringing, or learned it from a religious or other source. He may simply be reflecting that having penalized one child for a similar action he must act consistently when another child misbehaves in the same way. 'Act consistently' is itself a rule. It is worth emphasizing that it is not a rule which utilitarians need feel obliged to follow (even if, unthinkingly, they may do so). However similar the cases with which he is dealing, a utilitarian can feel free to apply different measures, so long as they seem to him to offer roughly equal chances of achieving deterrence, reform, or public protection.[6] It is only the retributivist who cries 'unfair'.

Some people will find this explanation of desert so uninspiring and pedestrian that it leaves them uncertain whether to discard the notion altogether or cast about for some new explanation that has not so far been offered. If so, something will have been achieved. My point is simply that this is the only way in which I can make sense of the notion of desert, and that if the sense it makes is so disappointing as to discredit retributivism, so much the better for utilitarianism.

Retributivists, however, have another shot in their locker. It is what Hart called 'retribution in distribution',[7] but in the next chapter I shall question whether this important principle need be seen as retributive.

11

The Negative Principle

ONE rule which is found in all developed criminal codes is what Hart calls 'the principle[1] of retribution in distribution'. In fact it consists of two rules:

1. nobody is to be penalized for an offence which he has not committed, attempted or planned. I shall sometimes refer to this as 'the wrong-person rule'.
2. the 'blameless-doer rule': nobody is to be penalized for an offence which he has committed without *mens rea*: that is, without intention or excusably.

The wrong-person rule is simpler to operate than the blameless-doer rule. If an offence has clearly been committed or attempted, the only question is whether A was the person who committed or attempted it; and if A is accused of being that person the question is usually decided by a court (or court-like tribunal), following rules of evidence. Apart from cases in which a miscarriage of justice is suspected, the only doubtful applications of the rule are those involving 'conspiracy'. People sometimes take part in the planning of an offence but dissociate themselves from the enterprise before it is launched. Some lawyers would regard them as proper subjects for punishment, others would not.

i. The blameless-doer rule

Unlike 'wrong-person' innocence, the blameless-doer rule has many applications, as the common law recognizes. The offender's act or omission may have been justified: self-defence is an example. It may have been excusable: he may have been acting under duress, or in order to survive. He may have made a mistake, for example by taking another man's raincoat for his own. He may have acted in one of the states called 'automatism', in which the body's movements are not willed (epileptic fits, sneezes, and sleep-walking are examples). He may have been under the influence of a mental disorder so severe that he cannot be blamed for what he did. He may simply have caused harm by accident. He may have been an under-age child.

Nearly all of these excuses are troublesome. Could the self-defender have escaped instead of assaulting his assailant? Was it necessary to kill him? If the excuse was duress, how severe was it? Does fear that one will be killed justify one in agreeing to kill someone else? If a man takes a raincoat without making sure that it is his own, is he really blameless? If he harms by accident, was the accident one that reasonable care would have avoided? If he was mentally disordered, was the disorder really so severe as to relieve him of any responsibility for what he did?

The most frequent problem is the under-age child. The Romans decided that children under the age of 7 should not be penalized. The Church adopted this as the minimum age for confession and penance. In pre-Norman England the minimum age for trial by ordeal was 14, but at some stage after the ordeal was replaced by juries it was reduced to 7, in line with the Church's practice, although the burden of proving *mens rea* lay upon the prosecution if the child was under 14. Over the last hundred years European and American countries have raised the minimum age, in some cases above 14, but in England only to 10. Even 10, however, is high enough to make a fiction of the assumption that no under-age child acts with *mens rea*. Modern minimum ages have little to do with *mens rea* and are really designed to protect children from criminal proceedings and penalties, on the assumption that these are unnecessary or will do them harm.

Only 'automatism' seems free of doubts. Yet like all the other forms of quasi-innocence it sometimes raises a question as to credibility. Can any man really strangle a healthy adult woman in his sleep?[2] It is credibility, too, which worries courts when duress, necessity, insanity, or mistake are pleaded.

What is more, even when the offender is excused for one of these reasons, utilitarianism often insists that something be done to him. When accidents of some kind are frequent and serious enough we make them offences: traffic law is an example. When professions suffer in reputation from the mistakes of their members, they discipline them for incompetence.

When the excusably insane seem dangerous we keep them locked up. When under-age delinquents are too much of a nuisance, or do serious harm, we apply restraints under civil law. The blameless-doer rule commands only grudging obedience, and is not allowed to endanger us.

This worries pure retributivists, of course. Since penalties for doing harm ought in their view to correspond in severity to the degree of the doer's culpability, zero culpability seems to preclude the imposition of unpleasant consequences. Utilitarians reply that this is precluded only if punishment is the sole kind of compulsory intervention that is regarded as justifiable. They point out that concern for the safety of others seems to justify such measures as quarantining innocent victims of dangerous diseases, or withholding driving-licences from some epileptics. If so, they see no reason why an excusable offence should not be regarded as justifying non-punitive intervention. The usual compromise between retributivists and utilitarians results in relegating compulsory intervention to civil proceedings,[3] so that it is not confused with punishment.

ii. 'Wrong-person' innocence

Where 'wrong-person' innocence is concerned, retributivists usually argue that the disagreement between them and utilitarians is too wide for compromise. Utilitarians, they claim, would be prepared to convict and punish the wrong person if this seemed to reduce the frequency of crimes. For example, if the clear-up-rate for murder were so low that it seriously weakened the deterrent effect of the penalty, would not the utilitarian be prepared to convict and punish someone for every murder even if this meant punishing the wrong people? Punishing the right people would obviously be preferable, since it would mean that fewer genuine murderers would be left at large; but when this was not possible would not punishing the wrong people be the next best thing?

Since this is one of the two big sticks with which retributivists beat utilitarians, it needs a thorough discussion. For example, it is based on three assumptions. One is that the wrong-person rule is so strict that any justification of punishment which allows it to be breached must be suspect. Another is that retributivism never breaches it. Both are questionable. In Chapter 13 we shall see (if we did not know it already) that in some cases punishing the undoubtedly guilty inflicts hardship or distress on the undoubtedly innocent. The retributivist, who believes (1) that punishing the guilty is morally obligatory but (2) that the innocent should never be punished is on the horns of quite a dilemma. He can try to saw off the second horn by arguing that the suffering of innocent dependants is not really punishment, because nobody *intends* them to suffer. Yet everyone concerned is aware that they will suffer. The distinction is a fine one: perhaps too fine. As we shall see in Chapter 13 the excuse offered for what I call '*obiter*' punishment is a lame one. The retributivist would be better advised to concede that the wrong-person rule is of the kind that admits exceptions. This would of course lead to breaches of the rule of consistency (see Chapter 12). If the normal penalty for a crime is imprisonment, should an offender who has a family be allowed to escape with a fine instead? The retributivist would have to draft exceptions to the consistency rule as well as to the wrong-person rule.

The retributivist's third assumption is that the utilitarian is *obliged* to punish innocent people when this would maximize the efficacy of law-enforcement. Is it an obligation or merely an option? Clearly it is an obligation for the utilitarian who is a 'maximizing utilitarian': the kind whose aim is to extract the maximum effect, in this case from a deterrent. The utilitarian who hedges, and says that it is merely an option which, as a non-maximizer, he would not choose, must be prepared to explain why he is hedging. Why is he content with something less than he could achieve? Why make an exception of the innocent? The retributivist will try to get him to admit that his only reason must be that the innocent do not deserve punishment; and that if he is a non-maximizing utilitarian he must be reasoning retributively.

iii. Non-retributive reasons

But must he? There are other possible reasons. For example, although Hart called the negative principle 'retribution in distribution', he pointed out that 'it has a value quite independent of Retribution as a Justifying Aim':

a *system* which openly empowered authorities to [punish the innocent], ... would awaken such apprehension and insecurity that any gain from the exercise of these powers would by any utilitarian calculation be offset by the misery caused by their existence ... [4]

If anything, this understates the argument. Even if attempts were made to keep the policy secret, in an 'open' society of the kinds with which we are familiar they would fail. Prosecutors or their staffs would leak, and the news media would soon publicize the existence of the policy. The public would become sceptical of the *bona fides* of most convictions, and would wonder how many of the real criminals were still at large. Deterrence would be minimized, not maximized. Scepticism would quickly become hostility to the whole system.

This is certainly arguable if one is living in an open society of the Western kind. Unfortunately it seems possible that in other kinds of society it would be quite easy to operate a secret policy which ignored the negative principle. All that would be necessary would be to adopt very low standards of proof and make it difficult for the defence to challenge evidence. It is not hard to think of examples of such regimes: China provided one in 1989.

iv. 'Fairness'

Yet there is another argument, which is neither retributive nor utilitarian. It uses Rawls's concept of 'fairness'. His concern is to define the sort of society that could be called 'fair'. He asks us to imagine a person who is non-altruistic (that is, who gives priority to his own interests). This person is pictured as being behind a 'veil of ignorance', not knowing whether he is to be incarnated as privileged, intelligent, and talented or as underprivileged, stupid, and incompetent. Nor does he know what stage of economic development has been reached by the hypothetical society into which he will be incarnated. Rawls argues that if he makes a rational choice he will opt for a society with a constitution and organization of a certain kind: roughly speaking, one that will offer equal opportunities of welfare and achievement to all its citizens. [5]

We might apply Rawls's rationale to the imaginary case of a person who is behind a similar veil of ignorance, but a more specific ignorance. He does not know whether he will be incarnated as a law-abiding citizen or as a law-breaker. In this case he is offered a choice between two societies which he is told differ in only one respect. Society N honours the negative principle; Society Q does not. In Society N he would be penalized only for offences for which he was genuinely responsible. In Society Q he would, if he found that he was incarnated as a law-breaker, be at risk of being penalized not only for his own offences but also for those which the authorities found it difficult to pin on anyone else. If he were incarnated as a law-abiding citizen he would be safe—from punishment at least—in Society N, but not in Society Q. The risk of being penalized 'unfairly' would not be large (unless the population of Society Q were very small), but it would make life in that society more apprehensive and insecure. It would also be a society in which the effect of deterrents would be minimized rather than maximized, at least if its potential law-breakers were as knowledgeable about its law-enforcement policy as our imaginary chooser. His rational choice, whether he is destined to be law-abiding or law-breaking, would be Society N, which from this point of view would be the 'fairer' of the two.

Rawls's non-altruistic man is not a utilitarian. The society which he would choose for its fairness is not necessarily the one which would have the lower crime-rate. Nor does Rawls's kind of 'fairness' involve the notion of desert: simply rational choice of a self-interested sort. The wrong-person rule need not be founded either on utility or desert.

v. Fairness and the blameless doer

Nor need the blameless-doer rule. Let Society S be a 'strict-liability society', allowing no excuses; and let Society B be one which applies the blameless-doer rule in the ways I have described. Our ignorant, selfish, rational chooser would quickly realize that his chances of being penalized would be considerably higher in Society S. He is not supposed to know whether he would be reincarnated as an offender or a law-abiding citizen; but he can certainly count on being reincarnated as a child. Only a completely unreal supposition might make the strict-liability society preferable: that excusable offences are much

more common than inexcusable ones, in which case it might be
a safer society to live in.

A retributivist might object that Society B is preferable only
because its blameless-doer rule is based on the notion of
culpability, and could not be operated by people who did not
understand the retributive concept of desert. But is this so?
Could it not be a society whose members simply disliked the
idea that they might be penalized for acts or omissions which
they could not help, and had framed their criminal code
accordingly? They need not see the blameless-doer rule as
honouring any retributive notion: only as maximizing each
individual's power to avoid being penalized. Expressed in
another and rather loose way, the rule provides that people are
to be penalized only for acts which they freely decide to
commit.[6] Thus Rawls's ignorant chooser would not necessarily
be preferring a retributively minded society: simply a society of
people who, like himself, wanted to minimize their chances of
being penalized involuntarily. From this point of view it would
be more precise to call the rule 'the involuntary-doer rule'.

vi. Hart and Rawls

At first sight these Rawlsian justifications of the wrong-person
rule and the involuntary-doer rule look like Hart's utilitarian
justification (quoted earlier in this chapter) expressed in a more
exact way. In fact there is a subtle but important difference.
Hart sees his preferred society as one whose members would
suffer less 'misery'. My Rawlsian chooser, however, would
prefer it not because it would be a happier society but because it
would minimize *his* chances of being penalized. Indeed it is not
certain that it *would* contain less misery than a society which
was prepared to breach these two rules. Its rates of serious
crime might well be much higher. The more scrupulous a
criminal justice system is in making sure that the people it
convicts did what they are accused of doing, and the more
sensitive it is to the excuses I have memtioned, the greater are
criminals' chances of escaping penalties. Hart's is a utilitarian
justification: my Rawlsian one is not.

Both are of course sociologically unrealistic. In real life
people honour the negative principle because they see it as

founded on desert, not on Hartian or Rawlsian reasoning. This chapter, however, is not a sociological discussion of people's beliefs. It is an answer to the question 'Could someone who rejects retributive reasoning nevertheless argue in favour of the negative principle?' The answer seems to be that he could. It follows that the rule-explanation of desert does not founder on the negative principle.

12

Commensurability and Proportionality

RETRIBUTIVISTS who have managed to explain desert to their satisfaction have still to solve another crucial problem: assessing the degree of severity with which offenders deserve to be punished. Two dimensions of this problem were mentioned in Chapters 8 and 9: the harm involved in the offence and the offender's culpability.

i. Harms

The harm, as we saw, may be done, attempted, or knowingly risked. The penalties for attempts used to be lower than those for successful crimes, and although this is no longer so in England, courts are still apt to take a more lenient view of them, illogical as this is. As for harms which are knowingly risked—for example by motorists who drive 'recklessly'—sentencers usually take a more lenient view of them if they do not actually happen (again the logic is questionable). If the risked harm does happen, the offender can plead in mitigation that he did not intend it; but the sentencer will want to know whether the offender believed it was certain to happen, very likely to happen, or merely a real possibility. Only the offender can reveal this, and he has good reason to lie.

Obviously some harms are graver than others. It is not hard to distinguish between death, bodily injury of a kind which results in a permanent disability such as the loss of an eye, and minor injury such as a bruise. Psychological harms present more difficulty, especially when the offence is a sexual one. So do offences of dishonest acquisition. If the victim is deprived of all his savings that is clearly more injurious than shop-lifting; but the range between them comprises innumerable differences. Often the sentencer's only yardstick is the value of the property: a very crude measure.

Sentencers could seek help from social scientists, who have studied the ways in which the public assess the seriousness of offences. Led by Thorsten Sellin and Marvin Wolfgang[1] they have found that samples of the population are able to assign numerical scores to descriptions of offences which vary such features as the injury or loss to the victim, the use or non-use of a weapon, the type of victim, and so on. Although respondents' ratings differ—for example with age and educational level— they show a fairly high degree of consistency, and make it possible to construct tables which not only range offences in rank order but also indicate by how much their ratings differ. Unfortunately (for our purpose) 'seriousness', as understood by respondents, took account of more than harm, so that, for example, 'forcible rape after breaking into a home' was ranked above 'assassination of a public official'. It might have been possible to induce respondents to think only of the harm involved when rating offences; but they could sensibly have retorted that they could not do so without much more information about the particular circumstances of the case. However that may be, for the present sentencers have to arrive at their own idiosyncratic estimates of the seriousness of harms.

ii. The second dimension

Culpability is even harder to assess than harm, especially if we accept the view of Fletcher and his followers that the proper target of blame is not simply 'the act plus the state of mind' but the moral character that made such an act possible. As we saw in Chapter 9 this is sometimes the only assumption that will make sense of excuses or pleas in mitigation. A striking example is the 'staleness' of an offence, which in some jurisdictions even protects the offender from prosecution. This can be justified only by reasoning that if the offence was committed a long time ago we cannot infer from it that the offender is still the sort of person who is capable of it. That is certainly arguable if the offender was very young at the time of his offence, but perhaps less plausible if he was in his twenties. And should we be thinking in terms of years or decades?

Evidence of good or bad character also gives rise to problems of relevance. The English Court of Appeal once reduced a prison sentence for a serious insurance fraud because the fraudster, while on bail, had jumped into a canal to save a drowning boy. Other appeals have succeeded because the offender had given a kidney to his sister, or founded a youth club. Spectacular behaviour seems to influence courts more than unobtrusive decency. More to the point, in none of these cases was the behaviour of such a kind as to suggest that the offender was not normally capable of dishonesty.

Even on the ordinary view that what is being blamed is not character but 'the act plus the state of mind', mitigation and aggravation are not easy to assess. Consider an example of provocation. A dislikes B, who taunts him about his lack of success with women whenever they meet. One day he responds by seizing a bottle by the neck and making to strike B. A friend grabs at his arm, and shouts 'Cool down: he's trying to provoke you'; but A struggles free and hits B with the bottle, continuing to do so after B falls unconscious to the ground. To what extent did B's provocative words mitigate A's culpability? Does A's previous dislike of B help his plea or tell against it? Should he have become used to B's taunts, or was the repetition of them a mitigating factor? Did he take in what his friend shouted about B's trying to provoke him, and if so should this have brought him to his senses? Should the fact that his friend tried to intervene have made him stop? Was the use of a bottle, and the repeated hitting of B, too excessive to be mitigated? As an English judge said long ago 'The Devil himself knows not the heart of man'; but without that knowledge trying to assess mitigating factors is like trying to unravel the Gordian knot with one's eyes shut.

Oddly, aggravating considerations seem slightly easier to handle. Premeditation is either proved or not. The same is true of professionalism, use of a weapon, misuse of a position of trust or authority. Previous convictions[2] are indisputable, although relevant only if it is character that is being assessed. Unlike most mitigating factors these do not involve surmises about states of mind at the time of the act. (One aggravating feature which does is the commission of a crime in a particularly sadistic way; but even in such cases the evidence is clearer than it is in most pleas for mitigation.) Any explanation of the difference must be speculative. It may be, however, that it lies in our criminal procedure. The prosecution is usually expected to prove aggravating features of the offence, during the trial, and these are therefore subject to the rules of evidence, whereas mitigating pleas are put forward by the defence after conviction, under relaxed rules of evidence and usually without challenge from the prosecution.

iii. The third dimension

The third dimension of the problem is seldom acknowledged by retributivists, although practical sentencers recognize it. Ironically it was Bentham[3] the utilitarian who tried to draw philosophers' attention to it, but without much success.[4] He called it 'sensibility', and although nowadays he would probably have used the word 'sensitivity' I shall continue to use his eighteenth-century term in order to emphasize its special meaning for penology. Bentham pointed out that the intensity of the suffering, hardship, or inconvenience which a given penalty will inflict depends on the individual offender: on sex, age, social position, and so on. Even if it is only a fine, and even when the amount of it is adjusted to take his means and his financial commitments into account, will it inflict hardship or mere inconvenience? What sacrifices will it force him to make? Or will he simply pass them on to his wife and children? If the penalty is imprisonment, how much does loss of freedom mean to him? How much will he mind the squalor of the gaol? Smith and Jones may be equally culpable accomplices: but a two-year sentence may make Smith suffer more than Jones. Sentencers know—or think they know—that women, the disabled, the very young, and people used to comfort suffer more than others from incarceration, but can only guess how much more in the individual case.

Even utilitarians may take 'sensibility' into account. Bentham realized that when penalties were justified only by the expectation that they would deter the offender (and not by the expectation that they would deter others) all that was justified was the minimum amount of suffering needed in his case; and that this varied from one offender to another. Women, children, and persons of superior social standing suffered more than ordinary male adults. Not all utilitarians need agree (and not all of Bentham's categories of sensibility would appeal to us nowadays). It is arguable that leniency in cases of special sensibility is likely to weaken the general deterrent effect of penalties. Ironically, Bentham's point should carry more weight with retributivists, who cannot ignore variations in sensibility, for the very reason that they mean that what makes one offender suffer as he deserves may make another suffer less or more than he deserves.

iv. 'Totality'

Sensibility complicates the arithmetic of retribution. If Smith commits two or more unconnected crimes on different occasions, retributive logic requires that the sentences for them should be consecutive: if they were concurrent he would get off too lightly. Yet English sentencers often make them concurrent, with the encouragement of their Court of Appeal. Their reasoning is based on what David Thomas has called 'the totality principle'.[5] If the addition of two or more sentences results in a total which is 'excessive' (to use the Court of Appeal's term) it must be reduced, preferably by making the sentences concurrent. In the many cases in which the Court of Appeal has used this ruling to shorten the totality there is no suggestion that it is utilitarian. If it is retributive it must be inspired by the notion of sensibility. (It is noticeable that most of the reported cases involve offenders who are either young or experiencing imprisonment for the first time.) The reasoning is almost certainly that the longer the total period of incarceration the less accurately does mere addition measure the suffering inflicted. Two consecutive four-year sentences are not simply twice as hard as a single one, but harder still.

v. Subjectivity

Even if the problems of culpability and sensibility could be solved, there would still be scope for disagreement about the appropriate dose of suffering for a given offence and a given offender. Smith and Jones, equally culpable and of equal sensibility, would nevertheless fare differently at the hands of retributive sentencers in Germany, Utah, and Pakistan. There is not, nor could there be, any standard by which one could say that German sentencers come closer than their Pakistani counterparts to achieving commensurability. This distinguishes sentencing from the trial of guilt. The justice of the latter can be assessed by comparing standards of proof: some systems clearly convict defendants on the basis of lower probabilities than do others. There is no such yardstick to tell us how commensurable a sentence is.

vi. Hegel's problem

Thus the unfortunate sentencer—or indeed any punisher—has to cope with a problem in three dimensions, none of which is measurable on any scale known to man. (And what notation does the Recording Angel[6] use?) He is like someone who is trying to define a position in space without any points of reference. For retributivists the likelihood of mistakes in determining the severity of punishment so as to fit the crime must be a major worry. As Hegel said, 'injustice is done at once if there is one lash too many, or one dollar or one cent, one week in prison, or one day, too many or too few.'[7]

vii. Proportionality

Hegel's solution was the abandonment of 'commensurability' for 'proportionality'; and according to Rupert Cross this is the approach of the English sentencing system. Proportionality, he wrote, is achievable

if the object is recognised to be a rough attempt to equate the size of the fine or the length of imprisonment to the gravity of the particular category of offence as contrasted with offences of other categories (theft contrasted with murder, for example) and the gravity of the circumstances in which the offence was committed as contrasted with those in which other offences of the same category are committed . . . [8]

Von Hirsch expounds it in more detail in *Past or Future Crimes*, but to the same effect. Most other authors do not distinguish it sufficiently from commensurability, perhaps because nobody nowadays regards precise commensurability as an achievable aim.

What the proportionalist envisages is two ladder-like scales whose rungs correspond. On the penalty-ladder each rung is meant to differ in severity from its neighbours. One awkwardness is that the degree of difference between Rung X and Rung Y cannot be assumed to be the same as that between Rung Y and Rung Z. A nine-month custodial sentence is more severe than a six-month one, and a six-month one than a three-month one; but are the differences equal? There are cases in which a short sentence does not lose a man his job when a longer sentence would. In this and other ways the measurement of the intervals on the scale depends on the circumstances of the offender. 'Overlap' too is a problem which is especially acute when a sentencer is hesitating between a custodial and a non-custodial sentence. The former is not always the more severe. Some offenders prefer a short time 'inside' to a heavy fine, and demonstrate this by deliberately defaulting. The rungs on the ladder are not merely loose: sensibility means that some are interchangeable.

The other ladder is equally rickety, although it could be improved with trouble. Its rungs consist of offences distinguished by their legal definitions: murder, robbery, rape, and so forth. This is crude because legal definitions do not distinguish degrees of harm with enough precision. There are murders and murders, robberies and robberies. Some robberies seem worse than some murders. Better would be a harm-ladder in which the rungs were well-defined harms. And since retributivists are concerned with culpability they ought to be not simply harms done but harms intended or knowingly risked. Yet if culpability matters, the rungs need to be elastic, so as to take into account mitigating or aggravating considerations. It is not surprising that proportionalists' descriptions of this ladder tend to be vague.

Fitting together two scales whose rungs are as loose and interchangeable as this is not as simple as the proportionalist makes it sound, and involves just as many considerations as attempts to achieve commensurability. The most he can claim is that sentencers who use his scales will be somewhat less idiosyncratic, and so somewhat more *consistent*, than they would without them. Consistency is a very formal virtue.

In fact all that most proportionalists seem to be proposing is a standard 'price-list' of a kind that will satisfy their public—or, if they are optimistic, educate it. Such a price-list needs no subtle gradations of harm, culpability, or sensibility: indeed they would confuse rather than satisfy or educate. This is utilitarian reasoning. Retributive reasoning would lead instead to a 'personal price-list' which would take into account not only gradations of harm but offender's culpability and sensibility. (This would not be an attempt to resurrect commensurability, since it would be based on the society's own price-list). Proportionalists who accept this could propose that the standard price-list in the shop-window would be subject to personal adjustments in practice; but if so the less the public is told about the practice the better.

viii. Utilitarians and proportionality

The retributivist can retort with a debating-point. His notion of proportionality may be crude, but the utilitarian, he may argue, has no sense of proportionality at all. His principles set no limit to severity, and make no attempt to equate it with the gravity of the crime or the culpability of the criminal. Historically, this is not quite true. Beccaria made two points.[9] First, if crimes of unequal gravity (his examples were assassination, poaching, and forging) are punished with equal severity this destroys people's ability to distinguish between their gravity. It is unfortunate for the utilitarian that there is no empirical evidence to support this. As we saw in Chapter 3 such evidence as there is makes it seem unlikely.

His second point was that if severity exceeds what is sufficient to achieve its purpose the excess is an evil without justification. Bentham[10] made the same point when he insisted that penalties must be 'frugal': no greater than is necessary to deter. The frugality principle is sound utilitarianism. It suffers from being rather theoretical, since in practice it is hard to tell when severity has reached the point of sufficiency, beyond which any increase would achieve no further decrease in the frequency of the offence in question. It seems to work in the case of capital punishment and murder, as we saw in Chapter 2; but it is not at all easy to tell whether increasing the normal length of prison sentences for, say, burglary by a year or two reduces the incidence of that offence. Even if this difficulty could be overcome, the result might well be a scale of penalties in which illegal parkers would fare worse than burglars—a result which would be quite unacceptable to those who believe that severity should bear some relationship to gravity. Modern philosophers[11] have so far failed to deduce from utilitarian principles a more acceptable sort of proportionality.

For the present, it seems, the utilitarian may have to slash at this Gordian knot. He can argue that if he wants his criminal justice system to be more than a pipe-dream—to work in practice—he must make it acceptable to his constituents. If enough of them are so retributively minded as to insist on some degree of proportionality between harm and penalty (with or without allowances for culpability and sensibility) that is what he must offer. He might perhaps get away with a system in which sentences which appear severe can in practice be lenient. Parole can have this effect so far as prison sentences are concerned, and fines can later be reduced without publicity. However that might be, this solution would be regarded by philosophers as not playing their game. Yet the utilitarian would not be inconsistent. He would simply be incorporating an acceptable proportionality into his system for political reasons, without believing in it himself.

ix. Consistency

Since consistency seems to be the only clear benefit which proportionality can be relied upon to promote, it needs a short discussion. It is certainly one of the criteria by which the public assesses the fairness of sentences. Inconsistencies are a frequent point of attack by the news media, and especially discrepancies between the sentencing policies of local benches of magistrates. Judges' inconsistencies are less striking, perhaps as a result of the efforts of the Court of Appeal; yet even that court has been known to contradict itself.[12] Magistrates sometimes defend inconsistencies between benches as justified by local crime-rates or economic conditions. Judges think less parochially. Their respect for consistency—or at least for the public's worship of it—is so strong that they sometimes refrain from imposing different sentences on accomplices even when there is reason to do so, for fear that this would discredit their policies.[13] And there have even been cases in the past in which the Court of Appeal has felt obliged to reduce a prison sentence which seemed to it fully deserved, because an accomplice had been sentenced more leniently by another court.[14]

This emphasizes the fact that consistency is only a conditional virtue. If there were such a thing as 'the right sentence' for a given offence, it would be possible to 'get it right' consistently; but also to get it wrong consistently. If one is not sure whether a fine of £100 is exactly 'right' for driving at 20 m.p.h. over the speed-limit a policy of varying the amount would increase the probability of 'getting it right' now and then. From a utilitarian point of view an appearance of consistency is politically wise; but sentencers' inconsistencies are what makes it possible for researchers to see whether one kind of penalty is more effective than another. Courts are seldom willing to randomize sentences deliberately, but the decisions of different sentencers in comparable cases are sufficiently varied to provide some scope for research of this kind.

If one is a sophisticated retributivist, however, consistency must have regard to all three dimensions of the harm–culpability–sensibility dimension. It is only a primitive sort which looks only to the legal definition of the offence, or only the harm done (or attempted, or knowingly risked). It is thus as difficult for a believer in commensurability to be sure of being consistent in two or more cases as it is to be sure of getting it right in a single case.

Only a sophist would use such points to discredit consistency completely. The believer in commensurability cannot claim to be able to sentence with consistent accuracy; but the proportionalist can claim that by striving for consistency he is at least maximizing proportionality within the limitations of the information available to him. And like the utilitarian he cannot afford to ignore the political risk which glaring inconsistencies would run.

13

Unintended Punishment

RETRIBUTIVISTS have other problems: the by-products of trial and sentence. Chief amongst these are unintended punishment and stigma.

i. Vicarious or *obiter*?

If the offender is a husband or father, wife or mother, imprisonment usually entails distress for an innocent spouse or child. This side-effect is well-known to probation officers and social workers, but few research workers have studied it.[1]

The hardship or distress inflicted in this way is sometimes called 'vicarious punishment': but that is a misnomer. Punishment is vicarious when its infliction on offenders' relatives or associates is deliberate. In the Old Testament Jehovah was not above visiting the sins of parents on their children; and some modern penal codes are not above penalizing parents for the delinquencies of their children. In war, or war-like situations, families or villages of guerrillas have been killed, usually to deter others from harbouring combatants. In peaceful conditions, however, the harm done to prisoners' dependants is not intentional: it is simply accepted as an unavoidable side-effect of legitimate punishment. It should be distinguished from deliberate vicarious punishment by calling it something else. 'Natural punishment' will not do, because that is the term used by Continental jurists to denote harms resulting from the crime itself: for example the injuries suffered by a bad driver or his companions. Perhaps '*obiter* punishment' will do.

ii. In practice

Since *obiter* punishment is regarded as a regrettable injustice, efforts are made to minimize it. English common law forbade the execution of pregnant women (and the Italian penal code still forbids their imprisonment, with exceptions[2]) because of the injustice that would be done to the unborn child. Modern sentencers often forgo a custodial sentence when the offender is the mother of a young family. The State recognizes an obligation to look after the finances of prisoners' families, and social workers are solicitous about their welfare. Housing authorities are sometimes prepared to maintain a prisoner's tenancy of his home. Probation officers offer group meetings to prisoners' wives and cohabitees, encouraging them to keep up contact with their husbands. Some prison systems (though not the British) allow 'conjugal visiting' which permits sexual intercourse.

All these expedients, however, are weak palliatives. Imprisonment almost always inflicts *obiter* punishment on someone. The only exceptions are families who are glad to be rid of the offender, and socially isolated men and women who are missed by nobody. Even fines, if heavy, may inflict deprivation on offenders' dependants as well as, or instead of, the offender. The retributive sentencer cannot escape the dilemma. With the exceptions just mentioned, a proportional (or commensurate) sentence inevitably inflicts some *obiter* punishment, which no amount of social work can cancel out. Those who object to utilitarianism because it seems to condone the punishment of the innocent (see Chapter 11) might ask whether the harm done every day to prisoners' dependants in the name of retributive sentencing does not amount to the same thing. Retributivists salve their consciences in two ways. They tell themselves—and sometimes the offender too—that he should have thought of his family before doing what he did. If they are more sophisticated they point out that the harm done to dependants is not intended by anyone, and so cannot, strictly speaking, be called 'punishment' (see the Introduction). Consolations, however, are not solutions.

Not that utilitarian sentencing avoids the dilemma. A deterrent or precautionary sentence is just as likely to inflict *obiter* punishment. True, the utilitarian is free to choose the minimum degree of severity that seems likely to deter, or protect, others; and this will sometimes be less severe than the sentence which would be dictated by proportionality (or commensurability). He may even be content with a fine or other non-custodial penalty when the retributivist would feel obliged to imprison. But he cannot be sure—the usual exceptions apart—that he is avoiding *obiter* punishment. Unlike the retributivist, however, he is not in a *moral* dilemma, because desert does not enter into his calculations. He may even reason that a moderate degree of *obiter* punishment will bring salutary pressure to bear on the offender: this seems to be the rationale of fining parents for their children's delinquencies.

iii. Incidental punishment

So much for vicarious, natural, and *obiter* punishment. There is another category: the direct but unintended. Its main effect is on the offender himself, but it is an effect which neither those who enacted the penal code nor those who administer it want the sentence to have. Perhaps 'incidental' will serve to distinguish it.

An obvious example is loss of one's job. A conviction does not always result in this; but a prison sentence nearly always does. An even more important example is stigma, which often makes it difficult for prisoners who have lost one job to get another after release. A conviction may stigmatize a person whatever his sentence, but a custodial sentence involves more serious stigma than, say, a fine or probation.

What is called 'labelling theory' even argues that stigma often increases the likelihood that an offender will reoffend. Not only may his difficulty in finding legitimate employment drive him into illegitimate ways of earning: rejection by law-abiding friends and relatives may drive him into the company of law-breakers, with obvious consequences. Being labelled 'dishonest' or 'violent' may even alter his image of himself to such an extent that he is more likely to behave dishonestly or violently.

We do not know how frequent such effects are.[3] Common sense tells us—and researchers confirm[4]—that the effects of stigma are less marked, or at least less keenly felt, when the offender has experienced more than one conviction. It is the stigma of the first conviction, or the first prison sentence, that is the most serious.

Efforts are made to limit stigma, but they are formal and half-hearted. Juveniles are fairly well protected in most Western countries, where they are usually tried in special courts, without spectators, and with a ban on the publication of any particulars that would identify them. Their stigma is limited to neighbourhood gossip. Adults fare less well. In some countries their convictions are officially expunged some years after they have occurred. In others they can apply for an official pardon, again after a considerable period. In Britain the more severe the sentence, the longer the offender has to wait before he can claim protection; and after a life sentence or a custodial sentence of more than thirty months he can expect no protection.[5] The only country known to me in which adults are to some extent protected like juveniles is Sweden, where the news media's code of practice usually does not allow them to be identified even in reports of their trials.

Utilitarians are not morally obliged to worry very much about stigma or other incidental punishments, although that does not exclude humanitarian misgivings (see Chapter 16). They may take into consideration the possibility that incidental punishment increases the chances of recidivism, if in the circumstances this seems at all likely. On the other hand they may think it more probable that stigma adds to the general deterrent effect of a sentence; and even, if the offender seems dangerous, that it warns other people to be wary in their dealings with him.

It is the retributive sentencer who is morally obliged to feel concern. If he is sentencing a man for his first conviction, should he adjust the sentence to take account of the fact that he has lost his job, and that stigma will make it harder for him to get another, or will impair his relationships with friends? Most sentencers would answer 'No: we cannot predict how severely, if at all, this will affect him. If we tried to take such considerations into account we might find ourselves choosing different sentences for two or more equally culpable accomplices in the same crime.'[6]

Yet if they ignore incidental punishment they are accepting the possibility, even the likelihood, that the totality of suffering, hardship, or inconvenience imposed on the offender as a result of conviction and sentence will exceed what they intend. What is more, since the ill-effects of incidental punishment vary from one individual to another, the totality will vary in a way that defeats the aim of proportionality (or even consistency). As was said in Chapter 12, the English Court of Appeal recognizes a 'totality principle' where consecutive sentences are concerned; but they have not extended it to cover incidental punishments. The moral dilemma, however, is inescapable for thinking retributivists.

14

Repentance, Reparation, Forgiveness, and Mercy

RETRIBUTIVISM has problems not only at its heart but also at its periphery, where it encounters notions such as repentance and forgiveness. Since it shared a childhood with them in the Judaeo-Christian world it cannot pretend not to recognize them now, even if their grown-up faces owe more to theology than to penology or philosophy. Theology is outside the scope of this book, but the secular versions of these concepts create minor awkwardnesses for moral philosophers, and especially for retributivists.[1] If one thinks one knows what a law-breaker (or a sinner) deserves, how should this belief be affected—if at all—when he is repentant, when his victim forgives him, or when mercy is urged? Does dealing with him mercifully mean that he gets less than his deserts? Can a consistent retributivist ever be forgiving, or merciful?

i. Repentance

Offenders are often said to be 'remorseful' by their counsel, and sometimes said to be 'repentant' by the prison chaplain. The distinction is worth making. Remorse is regret and self-blame for an act or omission, whereas repentance—especially in the Christian vocabulary—is the renunciation of a way of living or thinking. A criminal may be remorseful about some of his actions without contemplating the abandonment of his life-style. Remorse may gradually lose its *agenbite*, and eventually become no more than a remembered discomfort. Repentance must be kept up.

Sentencers are often urged to treat the offender's remorse as a mitigating factor. They may or may not believe in it. They are more likely to do so if he has shown signs of it, for example by trying to undo the harm he did (preferably before he knew he had been identified). They are less likely to believe in it if in court he pleads justification or provocation. As for pleading guilty, this is not nowadays regarded as a reliable sign of remorse: the explanation is more likely to be plea-bargaining or—in England at least—the knowledge that a guilty plea is likely to lead to a shorter sentence.[2]

Credibility, however, is not the main issue. Should genuine remorse persuade a sentencer to be lenient? If he is a utilitarian the question is simply whether a remorseful offender will be less likely to reoffend. The experienced sentencer may not be very sanguine. Remorse may be due simply to the special circumstances: for example the accidental injury to an elderly victim. It may fade too quickly. Some compulsive offenders feel remorse every time they do what they feel compelled to do, yet do it again. But the utilitarian who takes it into account is not being illogical—only optimistic.

For the retributivist the question is a different one. Should remorse mitigate culpability? It may, of course, be a fairly mild remorse, of the kind which amounts to little more than an acceptance of liability to punishment. At the other extreme, however, it may be of the bitterest and most lasting sort. If 'natural punishment' mitigates probably severe remorse should also. Perhaps repentance too is a reason for mitigation. This is easy to argue if one shares Duff's view (see Chapter 9) that the main justification of punishment is its power to induce repentance: the already repentant offender would then need no punishment (although Duff does not carry his argument so far as that). Even more weight must be given to repentance if one shares Fletcher's view (see Chapter 8) that what should be blamed and punished is not simply the act plus the state of mind but the character that was capable of so acting. If so, since repentance indicates an improved character, determined not to act in such a way again, it must point to considerable mitigation. If on the other hand the sentencer takes the usual view—that it is the act plus the state of mind for which the offender should be sentenced—it is less clear that simple repentance, unaccompanied by bitter, self-punishing remorse, should mitigate.

ii. Reparation

Reparation[3] is sometimes voluntary and disinterested—a spontaneous attempt to undo harm, or, if that is not possible, at least to express remorse. More often it is offered in the hope of dissuading the victim from complaining, or persuading the sentencer that remorse is genuine. More often still it is simply ordered by the sentencer himself. In strict legal theory this is the task of civil courts; but civil suits are so expensive, and delay payments so seriously, that western criminal courts are allowed to impose compensation on offenders. Unfortunately many offenders lack the means to compensate their victims adequately: hence the institution of compensation by the State. State compensation, however, is usually confined to crimes of physical violence and sexual molestation. Compensation for acquisitive offences is left to insurance companies; but large sections of the population—the young, the poor, the unbusinesslike—are not insured against such losses.

So sentencers face a variety of situations. Some present no difficulty. If the offender is affluent enough to pay compensation without hardship, all the sentencer need do is make a compensation order to make sure that he does pay, and then proceed to decide on the sentence. If the victim is eligible for compensation from the State or an insurance company the sentencer need do nothing but sentence. The same is true if the unlucky victim cannot expect compensation from any source. Slightly more difficult is the case in which the offender is in a position to pay adequate compensation but at the cost of considerable hardship to himself or his family. This may persuade the sentencer to reduce the severity of the penalty to take account of the hardship: a calculation which some sentencers seem able to manage.

The really awkward case for the retributive sentencer is one in which the penalty should clearly be imprisonment but the offender, who is the only possible source of compensation, can pay it only if he is left at liberty to draw his pay. Imprisonment will lose him his job, and make it unlikely that he will ever compensate the victim. A non-custodial penalty, on the other hand, will do less than justice. The utilitarian is less troubled by such cases, having to offer only pragmatic reasons for whatever choice he makes. For the retributivist, however, the dilemma is inescapable. He can try to side-step by arguing that the victim's need for compensation is the concern of civil, not criminal, law; but if the penal code empowers him to make compensation orders, that is no longer true. He may say that the fault is the State's for excluding such cases from its compensation scheme. But it is only an affluent Utopia that can afford to cover the losses of all uninsured victims. And to claim that there would be no dilemma 'if only . . .' does not dispose of it.

iii. Forgiveness

There are more spiritual problems, however, for the retributivist; and one concerns 'forgiveness'. If an offender spontaneously offers reparation, or shows clear signs of remorse, his victim's resentment may be lessened. If it is reduced to nil the result is called 'forgiveness', though not if it is merely lessened. Forgiveness does not seem to have degrees. If a victim forgives without any prospect of reparation, any apology, or other sign of remorse, this is regarded, especially by Christians, as particularly praiseworthy. It has been argued[4] that forgiveness is a virtue only if what is forgiven can be justified (or at least mitigated). Yet arguably the opposite is the case. If there was some degree of justification for it it is not 'forgivable' but 'excusable'; and if I commit such an act I am entitled to expect 'understanding' but to *resent* 'forgiveness'. True forgiveness is what is granted when the act is *not* excusable (or not wholly so). It is not owed, but bestowed.

'Who can forgive?' may seem an odd question to Christian readers, who would reply 'Anyone'. Yet it is possible to hold, as Jeffrie Murphy does, that forgiveness is possible only when one has resented something done to oneself:

To use a legal term, I do not have *standing* to resent or forgive you unless I myself have been the victim of your wrongdoing . . . . it would be ludicrous for me, for example, to claim that I had decided to forgive Hitler for what he did to the Jews. I lack the proper standing for this.[5]

Certainly it seems necessary, even for Christians, to differentiate between 'interested' and 'disinterested' forgiveness, even if both are virtues. Forgoing personal resentment is a different exercise from suppressing moral indignation. Why English, with its immense vocabulary, does not have two words for these two exercises is an interesting question.

But not as relevant as the question whether forgiveness, in either sense, is proper in a sentencer. 'Dieu me pardonnera,' said the dying Heine, 'c'est son métier.' But is it the *métier* of a judge or magistrate? Arguably not. If he feels personally injured he should not be the sentencer. As for 'disinterested' forgiveness, there seems to be no objection to his indulging in it while off duty; but his duty is to choose the sentence which is most appropriate from a utilitarian or a retributive point of view. If he thinks retributively he may take extenuating circumstances into account; but that, as we have seen, is not forgiveness.

iv. Mercy

Mercy is another matter, and must be clearly distinguished from forgiveness. Forgiveness is an attitude: mercy is an action. Like forgiveness it may be prompted by the offender's remorse or repentance, and one is more likely to be merciful if one forgives. But forgiveness does not oblige one to be merciful. Nor should a sentencer feel bound to be merciful because the offender's victim has forgiven him: if he did, he would be dealing inconsistently with the offender simply because he had been lucky enough to pick a forgiving victim. Conversely, mercy is not ruled out if the offender is not forgiven. If that were so, it would never be proper for sentencers to be merciful, since their duty does not include forgiveness.

It is arguable on other grounds, however, that sentencers cannot, or at least should not, act mercifully. Mercy is not the same as reasoned leniency. A sentencer, for instance, who reduces the penalty because the offender is already suffering from the consequences of his act is simply taking account of sensibility. If he reduces it because the harm intended was trivial he is merely honouring proportionality. If he deals lightly with a very stale offence it should be because he believes that the offender is no longer a person who is capable of such an offence (Fletcher's reasoning: see Chapter 8). If he is lenient because he regards the offence as to some extent excusable, he is simply thinking in terms of mitigation. If he refuses to apply a penalty such as capital punishment because in his view it should not be applied to any human being, he is obeying a humanitarian principle (see Chapter 16).

Alwynne Smart sees that if mercy is to have a place in secular penology it must mean something specific, but not reducible to the kinds of reasoning just described. She suggests[6] that we reserve the term for cases in which we justify leniency by appealing to 'the claims that other duties have on us'. The example she gives is the offender whose imprisonment would cause suffering to his family: our duty to them justifies us in not imprisoning him, even if he deserves it. (This is an interesting example, because it addresses itself to the dilemma faced by the retributive sentencer who sees himself as obliged to pass a prison sentence but knows that this will harm innocent dependants: see Chapter 13.) It might be objected that, attractive as it is, this solution reduces mercy to a mere rule for resolving conflicts of duties. The rule (which Smart does not spell out) might be to 'prefer the duty which protects the innocent', in which case it is an extension of the 'negative principle' discussed in Chapter 11. Or it might be to 'prefer the duty which involves the infliction of least harm', in which case it belongs to Benthamite utilitarianism. Either way, it seems to have lost some part of what we mean by 'mercy'. As Jean Hampton sees,[7] not a mere sense of duty but a sense of pity must be involved.

Yet if mercy is not merely a vague name for one or more of the kinds of justified leniency which I have been discussing, it is open to a serious objection from retributivists. It involves either not punishing the offender, or punishing him less than he deserves. As Jeffrie Murphy puts it, 'tempering is tampering'.[8] Retributivists are bound to wonder whether mercy has any place in a just penal system.

Oddly, philosophers who have recognized this problem have ignored the special sense in which the English penal system has for centuries used the word. 'The King's Mercy'—*misericordia regis*—was what sovereigns exercised when they interfered with judges' sentences. ('Mercy' is not merely a translation of *misericordia*, but a derivative of it.) Its modern name is 'the royal prerogative of mercy', but in republican countries it is recognized under other names: 'executive clemency' in the United States, 'la grâce' in France. Kant thought that only heads of state had this right, and only in special circumstances: but his odd ideas about those circumstances need not distract us. Although heads of state sometimes invoke it for improper reasons, as English monarchs occasionally did before Home Secretaries took control, its use is supposed to be prompted by mitigating circumstances,[9] and is not confined to the remission of the death penalty.

It was, and still is, a constitutional device for interfering with the penal system when the rigidity of the law prevents sentencers or other agents of the system from doing so. Any penal system which still has such points of rigidity needs a device of this kind, whether it is in the hands of the head of state or of an administrator. In Britain its use meant that it functioned in an important way. Some of the principles which governed it were eventually incorporated into the penal law. The use of the prerogative of mercy to commute death sentences which courts were obliged to impose on young murderers led to the legislation which laid down, and later raised, the minimum age for execution; and the practice of commuting death sentences on infanticidal mothers led to the Infanticide Acts which allowed judges to deal leniently with them. It thus had the additional function of promoting innovation.

If retributivists want to find a meaning and a role for mercy which distinguishes it from mere proportionality and the accepted conventions which regularly dictate leniency in the light of extenuating circumstances and the offender's sensibility, as well as from rules for resolving conflicts of duties, they could do worse than take this hint from history. 'Mercy' might well be reserved for extra-legal interference with the operation of too-rigid penal laws, when this can be justified. The justification would usually be some mitigating consideration not yet recognized by the accepted conventions of the courts. The exercise of mercy in this sense would not necessarily be a monopoly of heads of state or their civil servants. Probation officers could be called merciful when, for good reason, they do not bring probationers back to court for breaches of the requirements of their probation order. Prison governors who, again for good reason, grant more than the usual home leave to prisoners, could be called merciful. The same could be said of a magistrate who contrives to avoid convicting an offender, or imposing a compulsory disqualification, for instance by adjourning the proceedings *sine die*.

For utilitarians, however, mercy must have a different but equally precise meaning. Whenever an agent of law enforcement is faced with a choice between measures which he believes to be more or less equally effective, mercy is what he is exercising if he for good reason chooses the one which he believes likely to cause the least suffering to the offender. (It is always necessary to add 'for good reason' in order to exclude cases of favouritism or corruption.) He might even be called merciful if he made a choice which he believed to be *less* effective than another, simply because it would be kinder to the offender, although if he goes too far in this direction he might be called 'stupidly merciful'. What he does not have to worry about is the accusation that 'tempering is tampering with justice'.

PART IV
Attempts to Compromise

PART III must have demonstrated the difficulties and dilemmas which beset the genuinely retributive justification of punishment. The difficulty of explaining desert without recourse to metaphor, intuition, or superstition; the problems of proportionality; the dilemmas created by natural, *obiter*, and incidental punishment, amount to a formidable indictment. It is noteworthy that most 'just deserters' whose views have been discussed seem to have abandoned genuine retributivism and to be offering instead the notion that punishment is a message, justified by its hoped-for effect on the conduct of the offender or potential imitators. This is not so much a compromise with utilitarianism as a quiet conversion to it. But perhaps a genuine compromise is possible? The possibility is examined in the next two chapters.

Some compromises read well on paper, but fare less well in practice. Judges are the most practical, but are apt to leave loose ends. Philosophers are tidier with loose ends, but less practical. Academic lawyers' proposals are either very simple or very complex. Readers who feel that a compromise must be found will find at least one to their taste in Chapter 15 (if they find more than one they still have a problem). What Chapter 16 does is to draw attention to an approach which is neither utilitarian nor retributive, but which can dictate limits to both utilitarian and retributive policies. Humanitarianism has been mentioned here and there in earlier chapters (quite apart from C. S. Lewis's misuse of the term: see Chapter 7), and it is time to devote a whole chapter to it. Finally, Chapter 17 makes an all-important distinction between two kinds of compromise, and asks which kind, if any, is really forced on the utilitarian or the retributivist.

15

Jigsaw, Eclectic, and Hybrid Compromises

ONE sort of compromise is concerned with the justification of punishment, as distinct from the determination of its severity. Herbert Hart, for example, sees utility as the general justifying aim of the institution, but allows desert to play a part in deciding who is eligible for punishment (see Chapter 11), and whether its severity should be mitigated.[1]

A very similar compromise, but with elaborations, is offered by C. L. Ten.[2] Punishment is justified, he says, *if and only if*

1. the person punished is an offender who has voluntarily violated a legitimate law. (He calls this 'the retributive condition'; and it corresponds to Hart's 'retribution in distribution': see Chapter 11.)
2. punishing him is justified on utilitarian grounds (his 'utilitarian condition').

Although his second condition applies to punishment in particular cases it seems to imply that, like Hart, he sees utility as the justification for the institution of punishment also.

This is admirably clear and succinct. His 'revised compromise theory', however, complicates both conditions in interesting ways. Unlike Hart, he believes that there can be cases in which there would be considerable utility, and not too much harm to individuals, if innocent persons were punished. So he elaborates the first condition by adding

. . . or an innocent person whose punishment will inflict much[3] less suffering on him than the suffering that at least one other innocent person would have experienced as an additional victim of crime had there been no punishment.

Retributivists, that is, must be prepared to see what I called 'the negative principle' (in Chapter 11) not as absolute but as subject to exceptions dictated by utility.

This is particularly interesting because a non-absolute negative principle seems easier to accept if it is regarded not as a retributive principle but as a special version of Rawlsian 'fairness', in the way I have suggested in Chapter 11. Rawls's ignorant chooser might well be offered a choice between a society which punishes the innocent whenever this seems likely to reduce crime, and a society which does so only in the circumstances defined by Ten, in which case the latter would clearly be preferable.

Ten also feels obliged to modify his second condition. He sees, realistically, that there may be occasional cases in which penalizing the perpetrator of a crime has no utility; but he does not want to conclude that no penalty should be imposed in such cases. So he amends the second condition as follows:

punishing him does not have serious adverse effects on others, and punishing those who have voluntarily committed similar or lesser offences is justified on utilitarian grounds.

His example is a war-criminal who manages to escape punishment and live an idyllic existence, forgotten by everyone, on a desert island. No utility is achieved by punishing him: not even the satisfaction of a public demand.[4] Ten, however, does not want to conclude that he should be left in peace. He introduces the principle of consistency. Since punishing known war-criminals has utility, this unknown one must be punished too. We saw in Chapter 12 that the principle of consistency is not one which need appeal—or indeed should appeal—to a utilitarian, but must appeal to retributivists. So to fill the gap in his jigsaw puzzle Ten has had to insert another piece of retributivism.

He inserts yet another when he deals with the severity of penalties. The main consideration is of course that it must be sufficient to deter or incapacitate; but he believes that it must also be proportional to the gravity of the offence: a retributivist's stipulation. He sees the awkwardness of it: that proportionality may dictate penalties which are more severe than utility requires. Suppose that an offence of type X needs a penalty of severity S to reduce its frequency, whereas an offence of type Y does not, but is more serious because of the harm it may cause. Proportionality not only does not allow the severity of the penalty for Y to be less: it requires it to exceed S by an appreciable margin. Faced with a clear choice between proportionality and frugality Ten chooses proportionality.

That said, Ten's revised compromise is a thorough one, designed to deal even with cases which are rare but not inconceivable. What we now have to consider are compromises of the kind offered by writers who are not philosophers but practitioners, or at least participants in discussions of sentencing policy.

i. The eclectic sentencer

A compromise favoured by the English judiciary is of a kind which is best called 'eclectic', an adjective originally applied to the Greek philosophers who 'selected such doctrines as pleased them in every school'.[5] The best-known exposition of judicial eclecticism in England is David Thomas':[6]

The Primary Decision
The effect of this legislative structure is to create two distinct systems of sentencing, reflecting different penal objectives and governed by different principles. The sentencer is presented with a choice: he may impose . . . a sentence intended to reflect the offender's culpability, or he may seek to influence his future behaviour by subjecting him to an appropriate measure of supervision, treatment or preventive confinement. In some instances both objects may be pursued simultaneously and find expression in the same sentence, but more frequently this is not possible. Achievement of the broader objectives of a punitive sentence may require the sentencer to adopt an approach which is not likely to assist the offender towards conformity with the law in the future, and indeed may positively damage such prospects of future conformity as exist already, while a measure designed to assist the offender to regulate his behaviour in the future may appear to diminish the gravity of the offence and weaken the deterrent effect of the law on potential offenders.

The sentencer's 'primary decision' is whether to impose a 'tariff' penalty intended to reflect the offender's culpability, or an 'individualized'[7] measure with a utilitarian aim. A tariff penalty is not necessarily of course imposed for retributive reasons. The sentencer *may* have a utilitarian objective, and may believe that in the circumstances of the case a tariff sentence is preferable to an individualized one because it will deter potential imitators, or because its deterrent effect is more likely than an individualized measure to persuade the offender himself to obey the law he has broken. Yet, as Thomas's reference to culpability confirms, tariff sentencing is more likely to be based on a retributive approach.

Consequently the judge who hesitates between a tariff and an individualized sentence is usually wondering whether to deal with the case in a retributive or a utilitarian way. The point is that he believes he has a choice. So too, of course, does a sentencer who is an uncompromising utilitarian. He may ask himself whether he is more likely to contribute to the reduction of crime by passing a deterrent sentence or by placing the offender under supervision, or under some form of precautionary detention. But his choice is between expedients and not approaches. He is not an eclectic in the same sense as a colleague who sees himself as having a choice between inflicting deserts and reducing crime.

Even his colleague may not always see himself in that clear light. If the tariff tells him that the sentence in the case must be one of imprisonment, and that the normal range is between a minimum of X and a maximum of Y, he may settle on the exact term without asking himself whether his main consideration has been retribution or deterrence[8] (or indeed mere consistency with the policy of his colleagues). Yet if the offender's culpability bulks large in the sentencer's thoughts he is reasoning retributively, and if he is an eclectic he will not feel that this debars him from passing a utilitarian sentence in another case.

ii. Emotional eclecticism

What seems very hard to defend is what can fairly be called 'emotional eclecticism'. Some sentencers reason in a utilitarian way until they encounter a case which so shocks them that they resort to retribution. Sadism, callousness, extreme greed, treachery, or the selection of victims who are handicapped by age, youth, or disability, are apt to elicit sentences with homilies about desert. It is as if there were what psychologists and engineers call a threshold: when culpability rises above it, a different sort of reasoning is switched on. The threshold, however, is idiosyncratic. For some sentencers it is low, for some quite high. If inconsistency is a defect in a sentencing system, one way of promoting it is emotional eclecticism.

If inconsistency were the only objection, however, it could be reduced to an acceptable level by an eclecticism which obeyed rules—if an acceptable set of rules could be formulated. There are several ways in which this might be done,[9] some more attractive than others.

iii. A two-tier rule?

A simple solution would be possible if offences against the criminal law could be divided into two groups, one to be punished retributively, the other to be penalized in merely utilitarian ways. Many jurisdictions make broad distinctions between offences according to the degree of disapproval which they arouse. The French distinguish three kinds: *crimes*, *délits*, and *contraventions*. The Scots distinguish crimes and offences. England used[10] to distinguish felonies and misdemeanours, and the United States continues to do so. None of these distinctions, however, carries the implication that only the more serious categories call for retributive punishment.

An implication of this kind might be read into the old jurists' distinction between *mala in se* ('things that are wrong in themselves') and *mala prohibita* ('things that are (merely) forbidden (by laws)'). Retributive reasoning could be confined to the former (in theory of course, because it is not easy to prevent a sentencer from being influenced by notions of desert when he is sentencing for a regulatory offence: the most that could be hoped for would be that a declaration of the rule would make this less frequent). The rule, however, would satisfy few people. In the first place it would need to be supplemented by a list of *mala in se*, and the arguments about what this should and should not include would be endless. More important, retributivists would argue that people who knowingly and intentionally commit *mala prohibita* are often as culpable as those who commit *mala in se*, especially when the prohibitions are clearly meant to protect others from serious harm.

iv. A priority rule?

If we abandon—as surely we must—the idea of distinguishing between kinds of offences, we must resort to some rule of priority that will tell sentencers whether and when to pay more attention to utility or desert. The simplest rule would be that the sentencer should choose the objective which is most likely to be achieved. This was the proposal of the Supreme Court of Victoria:

The courts must continue to balance deterrence, rehabilitation and retribution but it must be recognized that where it is not possible to have much or any confidence that the sentence imposed will do anything by way of deterrence or rehabilitation, substantial retribution must be exacted. The legal system must exact retribution from an offender because otherwise the community in the last resort will exact its own. In a civilised society that is not acceptable.[11]

In other words, sentencers should aim at deterrence or rehabilitation, except when they have little confidence that they will achieve either, in which case they should fall back on retribution. It is a pity that the Supreme Court forgot—or decided not—to mention incapacitation, since this is something which sentencers can usually be confident of achieving by custodial sentences of sufficient length; but that would have complicated matters! The Supreme Court's stated reason for insisting on retribution is essentially pragmatic: otherwise, they argued, the community would exact unofficial retribution. It is not clear whether they believed in retribution for its own sake, and merely threw in this argument by way of reinforcement (in which case why is retribution relegated to a 'fall-back' position?), or simply regarded the public's belief in retribution as something which courts ignore at their peril. In spite of these defects, however, their proposal makes sense. It would of course lead to some sentencing decisions that would outrage a retributively minded public. Sentencers are occasionally bold enough to use probation—with or without psychiatric treatment—for crimes of serious violence which, in the public's view, call for retribution; but if the sentencer is persuaded that probation will 'rehabilitate', that is what the Supreme Court says he should do.[12] Or he might incapacitate a non-violent but repetitive burglar with a twenty-year prison sentence, again outraging public opinion; which is, perhaps, why the Supreme Court were silent about public protection.

v. Hybrid compromises

Less pragmatic, perhaps, but more precise, is the proposal by Paul Robinson, a dissident member of the United States Sentencing Commission.[13] After discussing other possibilities (though not all of them) he suggests a rule which would allow desert to be 'the determining principle' and utility only a limiting principle. Sentencers would be expected to choose sentences which are retributively appropriate *unless* the result would be an 'intolerable' increase in the crime-rate, in which case they could be more (or, presumably, less) severe, *but not to an extent* that would be 'intolerably unjust': that is, intolerably more severe than the offender deserved. Note that the rule makes sense only if it prescribes a sentencing *policy*, not if it is regarded as a guide for a sentencer when he is dealing with an individual case. No single sentencing decision could be regarded as at all likely to result in an intolerable increase in the crime-rate.

vi. Utility limited by desert?

As Robinson points out, this rule could be stood on its head. Sentencers could be enjoined to sentence with utility in mind, unless the result would be a sentence which is 'intolerably unjust' from a retributive viewpoint. This is what Lord Longford proposed in *The Idea of Punishment*, followed some years later by Norval Morris in *Madness and the Criminal Law*.[14] It is sometimes called 'limiting retributivism'. Essentially, it treats retribution not as a duty but merely as a rule that sets upper limits to the severity of punishment (its supporters do not talk about lower limits, because it is an effort to present retributivism as a benevolent philosophy). Most British penal statutes are drafted on what could be interpreted as this principle.[15] They specify upper limits to the duration of custodial sentences, the amounts of fines, the hours of community service, and even the duration of probation: all that is missing is an explicit declaration that within the limits the sentence should be determined by utilitarian considerations. (In practice the limits often serve merely as checks on the retributive feelings of some sentencers.) In some other countries—notably the United States—statutes may also specify lower limits for custodial sentences.

Strictly speaking, not all these solutions are 'eclectic'. Some are 'hybrid', because instead of allowing sentencers to switch from utilitarian to retributive principles they graft the two principles together. But that is merely a point for the taxonomist. What the solutions demonstrate is that eclecticism need not be merely emotional: that it can be rational. The *mala in se* solution is of course academic nowadays, when few people would be prepared to endorse black and white lists of *mala in se* and *mala prohibita*. Robinson's solution—desert modified by utility limited by desert—also verges on the academic: the difficulties of estimating the effect of desert on utility, and of deciding what is 'intolerable', are too great.

The 'priority solution'—sentencing for utility, and taking desert into account only when no utility seems achievable—is not academic; but it is unlikely that all its consequences could be made acceptable to the public, especially when the probable reactions of the news media are borne in mind. If this objection is ignored, however, it has some appeal for one sort of utilitarian: the sort who is not so repelled by retributive reasoning that he will reject it even when utility seems unachievable.

Longford's solution, which allows desert to be no more than a limiting consideration for utilitarian sentencers, does not face the point made by the priority solution. There are cases in which no utility can be expected from any sort of sentence. The Supreme Court of Victoria's remedy was simply to concede that in such cases there is nothing left but desert to determine what the sentence should be. Ten's remedy is to say that the sentence should be consistent with sentences which, in similar cases, do have utility. This seems to improve on the Supreme Court's remedy, even if the consistency rule belongs to retributivism.

Longford's solution does not, of course, escape the difficulties with which retributivism has to struggle. And it intensifies the central difficulty of explaining the nature of desert. For the pure retributivist, desert is something that *ought* to be inflicted. But when desert is relegated to the status of an upper[16] limit it becomes something which it is merely *permissible* to inflict. This makes it even harder for the retributivist to explain it in any of the metaphorical[17] ways which were outlined in Chapter 9. If it is a debt it *ought* to be paid in full. If it is what annuls harm, literally or symbolically, it must be whatever is needed to do so. The same seems true if it is regarded as the removal of an unfair advantage. And if it is a message it must be *delivered*. All these metaphorical explanations were devised by and for retributivists who saw the infliction of desert as obligatory. The only explanation which is reconcilable with the notion of desert as an upper limit to severity is the rule-explanation offered in Chapter 10.

Finally, Longford's solution makes two assumptions of which neither is quite true. The first is that utilitarianism includes no principle which sets limits to severity; and, as we saw in Chapter 12, the frugality principle does set limits, even if in practice it is very hard to tell when severity has reached those limits. The second assumption is that the only philosophy capable of setting limits is retributivism. But what about humanitarianism? This is the subject of the next chapter.

16

Humanitarian Limits

LONGFORD's compromise may therefore not be the last word. We might grant that there should be some principle which sets limits to the severity of what simple utilitarians might want to do, and yet we might question whether it need be the retributive principle.

i. Utility and limits

Sometimes utility itself points to limits. Penalties can be so severe that juries will hesitate to convict even defendants who are clearly guilty, as sometimes happened in English nineteenth-century trials when grand larceny carried the death penalty. Today in the United States when a capital case comes up for trial, jurors have to be cross-examined to make sure that the jury will be 'death-qualified': that is, will include nobody whose views on capital punishment would compel him to hold out against conviction. Researchers have found that this produces a selection of jurors who are 'more likely to trust prosecutors and distrust defense attorneys, consider inadmissible evidence even if a judge instructed them to ignore it, and infer guilt from a defendant's silence'.[1]

Even non-capital penalties may be so severe as to be counter-productive. Where the penalty for theft is loss of a hand, even victims and courts hesitate to invoke the law. Very long sentences engender sympathy for offenders, even amongst people who do not know them.[2] They may make men unfit for useful employment, and impose material and psychological deprivations on their families. Minimum sentences are less often regarded as counter-productive, but may be. Fines may be so tolerable that offenders who can afford them treat them as mere taxes, for example on illegal parking.

ii. Humanitarian limits

Only a very simple utilitarian could ignore such doubts. The point of this chapter, however, is that upper limits can be advocated on grounds that are neither utilitarian nor retributive. The best term for such grounds is 'humanitarian'. It is a fact of history that it has been humanity, not notions of utility or desert, which has inspired opposition to the death penalty, attainder, loss of civil rights, castration and other mutilations, flogging, transportation, and solitary confinement. The humanitarians were not the policy-makers who agreed to abolish these measures (their motive was political expediency) but those who campaigned for abolition. No doubt some of them saw their cause as utilitarian, or at least employed utilitarian arguments, not always wisely. But their underlying motive was humanitarian: a feeling that such things should never be done to human beings.

iii. Human rights

Humanity, as the Stoics recognized, must not be confused with mere kindliness towards children, relatives, or friends. It is an acknowledgement of the fact that human beings who have no connection with us deserve the same consideration (although not all the Stoics were so sure about slaves or barbarians).[3] How much the early Christians contributed to what we would call humanitarianism is debatable; not much, thought Lecky.[4] It was the Roman lawyers of Byzantium who developed the notion of a 'natural law' which applied to all mankind. At first it was seen as consisting mainly of duties and obligations, but in the Middle Ages it gave birth to the concept of 'natural rights', which (in spite of Bentham's scepticism) inspired the English Radicals, the French Revolutionaries, and the American Declarers of Independence. The 'rights of man'—nowadays called 'human rights'—provided Western civilization with a formal way of talking and reasoning about humanity.

Not that humanitarianism is dependent on a belief in human rights. Plenty of people preached humanity before human rights were invented (or 'discovered', if you believe in 'natural' rights). Bentham himself regarded natural rights as 'nonsense on stilts', but—as we saw in Chapter 12—preached 'frugality' in the severity of penalties: that is, the principle that their severity should be limited to the minimum needed to achieve their purpose. In his case the principle was an integral part of his utilitarianism, since his 'felicific calculus' meant that a penalty which exceeded the necessary severity had unnecessarily diminished the total of human happiness. It seems possible, however, to believe in the frugality principle without being a utilitarian; and if so the belief is humanitarian. As for rights, humanitarianism can prompt actions which people cannot claim as of right. Philanthropy offers many instances. Conversely, a humanitarian who believes that we have a right to do certain things—such as execute murderers—can also hold that humanity forbids it. Even those who do not speak the language of rights draw the line at doing some things to their fellow-men. Nils Christie is an example. His book on criminal justice, *Limits to Pain*,[5] justifies his proposals by the simple objective of 'reducing man-inflicted pain on earth', but without appealing to the notion of human rights.

iv. The language of rights

Nor has the language of rights been particularly effective in securing the reduction of 'man-inflicted pain'. Even states which have subscribed to constitutions or conventions forbidding penalties that are 'cruel and unusual'[6] or 'inhuman or degrading'[7] do not seem to have felt obliged to modify their penal codes as a result.[8] There was a time when it seemed that the use of the death penalty in the United States would be declared 'cruel and unusual', but this was avoided by new statutes which made the choice of execution a matter of jury discretion. In Europe and the rest of the world, states which have abolished capital punishment have done so not in obedience to constitutions or international conventions but in response to less formal, less definable, pressures. It is even arguable that the language of rights has provided a euphemism which enables diplomatic discourse to gloss over the raw reality of summary executions, torture, enslavement, and other forms of oppression which take place daily in many countries. 'Violation of human rights' is so colourless a phrase that it seems almost designed to arouse the minimum of indignation.

Nevertheless, where punishment is concerned, the language of rights makes it easier for humanitarians to state their case with some degree of precision. They seem to be saying

1. that there are some forms or degrees of severity which are so 'cruel' or 'inhuman' or 'degrading'[9] that people have a right never to be subjected to them;
2. that they have this right regardless of what utility or desert seems to dictate.

And Bentham would have added (if he had used the language of rights)

3. that they have a right to be penalized with no more severity than is strictly necessary for utilitarian purposes.

It is the second and third of these claims which are the main point of this chapter. Plainly even countries which subscribe to Claim 1. can interpret 'cruelty', 'inhumanity', or 'degradation' in their own ways (just as they can interpret 'desert'). The point is the possibility of claiming that the form and severity of punishments should be subject to limits which are different from those based on utility or desert. In more concrete terms, it is possible for a humanitarian to concede that the death penalty is deserved in many cases, and that it is equal to, and cheaper than, any other penalty as a general deterrent, and nevertheless to assert that it is ruled out because it is too inhumane, or more severe than is necessary.

v. The need for nouns

Moral principles, however, are not very effective without rules that tell us how they are to be applied in practice;[10] and even when rules are offered, as they are in the United States' Constitution or in the international conventions, they may fail to do their job. In those cases they fail because they are drafted in terms of adjectives instead of nouns. Banning what is 'cruel', 'inhuman', or 'degrading', without saying what sorts of measures merit these adjectives, has had little if any effect on penal practice. Only when humanitarian campaigners have used nouns, and specified practices such as capital punishment, flogging, or solitary confinement have they had any success.

To return, however, to the point of this chapter: could a utilitarian who is prepared to accept non-utilitarian limits to penalties seriously consider humanitarian limits instead of retributive ones? He would certainly find humanitarian limits more restrictive in the case of offences for which retributivists would be prepared to allow capital or corporal punishment or long confinement under harsh conditions. They would be less restrictive, however, when he was considering penalties for the commoner and less serious offences. There is nothing inhumane about disqualifying an able-bodied motorist from driving; and it would be a powerful deterrent for illegal parkers: but most retributivists would regard it as going beyond the bounds of desert for that offence, and most utilitarians would argue that there are more 'frugal' ways of keeping the offence within tolerable bounds.

The utilitarian might well be attracted by the freedom which merely humanitarian limits would allow him; but he would have difficulty in persuading a retributively minded public that desert should be disregarded. He would have even more difficulty over culpability. A humanitarian can take account of sensibility, and set more restrictive limits to penalties for children or invalids, for example; but he cannot take account of culpability without thinking like a retributivist. A retributivist's limits vary if mitigating or aggravating facts are established. The humanitarian principle takes no account of them.

I say 'the humanitarian principle' rather than 'humanitarians' for the sake of precision. A humanitarian does not necessarily reject retributive reasoning: he may believe that the severity of penalties should be limited by both desert and humanity (and indeed by utility). And the utilitarian who thinks politically, debating with himself what sort of penal code he could make acceptable to his public, would be well advised to allow both retribution and humanity—or, more precisely, the retributive and humanitarian views of his public—to modify his plans. What I have been discussing in this chapter, however, is the humanitarian principle in its pure formulation, in order to see what a penal code would be like if it relied on nothing else to restrain the utilitarian.

17

Why Compromise?

THE hunt for compromises, though popular, overlooks an important difference between two sorts. One is merely political. It is devised and proposed in order to attract support from constituents, and its features are determined not by logic but by its proposers' beliefs about the preferences of those constituents. There are signs of political compromise in some of the proposals of modern retributivists, especially those who suggest that punishments are justified because they are moral messages of an influential sort. The fact that such evidence as there is points in the opposite direction[1] has not discouraged them.

Utilitarians too may have to offer a political compromise when faced with the problem of proportionality, as we saw in Chapter 12. But we also saw that it need not be an intellectual compromise. It is only acceptability which *obliges* them to concede that severity should be graded so as to accord with the gravity of the offence. If enough of their constituents were full-blooded utilitarians, or could be induced to believe that the more culpable offenders are in practice penalized more severely than the less culpable,[2] they could make their sentencing systems acceptable and therefore workable. They do not have to believe in proportionality themselves.

i. Intellectual compromises

The other kind of compromise is intellectual, and does entail a shift in one's own beliefs. It is necessary only when each party's position suffers from at least one defect which cannot be remedied without help from the other. If only one of them has such a defect the other side need not negotiate, and wins, as it were, by default.

Utilitarianism is usually supposed to suffer from two such defects. One is its difficulty in providing proportionality of a sort that would be acceptable to retributively minded constituents;

but, as we have seen, the utilitarian need offer only a political compromise to deal with this. The other is his alleged inability to justify the negative principle that innocent persons and 'blameless doers' should not be penalized. Hart, however, has suggested a utilitarian justification for this principle, and I have suggested a Rawlsian one which seems less open to objection than Hart's (see Chapter 11).

Proportionality and the negative principle apart, utilitarians need only be careful not to make over-optimistic claims for the efficacy of their techniques. Moral messages have not been shown to have any desirable influence, and such evidence as there is suggests that they are in fact ineffective. Corrective techniques probably work in some cases, but these cases are difficult to identify in advance, and sentencers cannot be sure that they will be applied as they are meant to be. General deterrents are certainly not ineffective, although their effect has been both denied and exaggerated. Incapacitating measures— especially of a custodial sort—are undeniably effective for as long as they are allowed to last.

Moral objections have not so far been raised to the use of penalties as messages, and it is unlikely that they will be until such messages are shown to be influential. Moral objections to deterrents, as we saw in Chapter 6, are rhetorical rather than real. The same is true of C. S. Lewis's attack on attempts to improve people's characters. Moral objectors to incapacitation seem to beg questions that must not be begged or to commit outright fallacies, of the kind dealt with in Chapter 8.

It is retributivists whose position seems to have irremediable weaknesses. As we saw in Chapters 9, 12, and 13, they can give only lame answers to crucial questions. How is the obligation to inflict desert to be explained? How is the three-dimensional problem of commensurability to be solved? (Certainly not by 'proportionality'.) Can the dilemmas posed by *obiter* and incidental punishments be ignored?

The Argument

I INTRODUCED my argument by outlining the seven features of the Western conception of punishment, but avoided defining it in a question-begging way. The question which must not be begged is 'Should our justification for what we officially do to offenders be utilitarian or retributive?'

The predominantly utilitarian outlook of British and American judges and policy-makers has been threatened lately by a revival of retributivism, or, more precisely, a version of it called 'modern retributivism' or 'just deserts'. There is a difference. Classical retributivists saw the infliction of deserts on offenders as a duty, modern ones as a *pis aller*. Scepticism about the attainability of utilitarian aims, coupled sometimes with moral objections to them, have disillusioned penologists and philosophers to an extent that has made them fall back on an objective which seems less open to doubts.

Part I suggests, however, that the scepticism was the consequence of exaggerated interpretations of the empirical evidence. This showed, for example, that general deterrents influenced fewer people, and under more limited conditions, than we used to think: but not that it never worked. Again, attempts to correct the offenders themselves are handicapped by the difficulty of telling which offenders are likely to respond, and to what sort of corrective, plus the equal difficulty of ensuring that they get that corrective: but to claim that no corrective measures ever work is going too far.

Elimination and incapacitation unquestionably work, although they demand a greater degree of ruthlessness. What has no support from the evidence is the hope that penalizing offenders will have desirable effects on the public's moral attitudes, or will at least provide it with a satisfying ritual. What little evidence research has supplied casts doubt on this.

If an objective is obviously or probably unattainable, and attempts to attain it involve the imposition of suffering, hardship, or inconvenience, this in itself amounts to a conclusive moral objection to those attempts. But since this is not true of all utilitarian objectives there are more specific moral criticisms to be considered, some applying to deterrence, some to correction, some to elimination or incapacitation. Part II discussed them, but found them either weak or downright fallacious.

Part III examined thoroughgoing retributivism, classical and modern (compromising versions being left to Chapter 15). Essential to any version is the notion of blame, and its complications were the subject of Chapter 8. Even more central, however, is the problem of explaining why there should be a moral obligation to inflict desert; and, as Chapter 9 showed, retributivists' attempts to solve this have serious defects. Chapter 10 suggested a solution which they might consider, but which is unlikely to appeal to them, since it reduces the obligation to mere rule-following. Moreover, they could argue that the principle of 'retribution in distribution', which forbids the penalizing of the innocent, does not fit the rule-theory. To call it 'retribution in distribution', however, begs the question whether it really is a retributive principle. Certainly most people would justify it by saying that the innocent do not deserve to be penalized. Yet it is possible to found it not on the notion of desert but on the Rawlsian notion of 'fairness'. This being so, it does not falsify the rule-theory.

Retributivists, however, have other problems to solve. They may claim that it is easier to be certain of inflicting desert in a given case than it is to be certain of achieving any utilitarian objective. But this is only roughly true. Hegel pointed out that one lash too many or too few makes the punishment unjust. Unless this is dismissed as a quibble, retributivists must tell us how to be sure that a penalty is neither too severe nor too lenient. 'Commensurability' of the kind which the Recording Angel would certify is unattainable. The best that modern retributivists can offer is 'proportionality'—a ladder with rungs that are both sliding and elastic. The certainty it promises collapses in practice.

Retributivists have peripheral problems too, although they are not always acknowledged. 'Vicarious' punishment can simply be dismissed as improper; but that does not dispose of cases in which punishing the offender himself imposes foreseeable suffering on his dependants. And since incarceration entails stigma and loss of employment for at least some offenders, sentencers are faced with a dilemma. Should they adjust the official penalty to take this into account, and if so by how much? Or should they ignore these unintended but inevitable effects? If one is a retributivist the choice is between the unquantifiable and the indefensible. As for repentance, forgiveness, and mercy, they too can be ignored by hard-hearted retributivists, and indeed are ignored by most. If they are not ignored they raise minor problems—but only for retributivists.

Finally, Part IV discussed compromises that have been proposed with a view to reconciling utilitarians and retributivists. The most popular allow utilitarians to dictate objectives but retributivists to dictate upper limits to severity. What Chapter 16 pointed out was that it is not only retributivism that can set limits of that kind: humanity too can do so, although its limits may operate rather differently. The all-important question, however, is whether either utilitarians or retributivists can do without a compromise. Chapter 17 considered this, and made the crucial distinction between political and intellectual compromises. The utilitarian must accept at least one feature of retributivism—proportionality—if his policy is not to be sabotaged by constituents who think retributively. But this is merely a political compromise: he need not enter into an intellectual one. The retributivist, on the other hand, is obliged by more than one irremediable weakness in his position to compromise intellectually.

This does not mean that retributivists are completely routed: only that they must retreat to ground where they are less open to attack—their right to have retributive feelings. Not many people, when confronted with some kinds of misbehaviour, can honestly deny any desire that the misbehaver should suffer. Some people have been trained to feel guilty about desires of this sort, and a few have been so well trained that they do not feel them. (Nietzsche[1] was at such pains to condemn feelings of this kind that one is tempted to look for a psychoanalytic explanation.) Even utilitarians need not disown them. Like Bentham they can acknowledge the 'pleasures of malevolence' without guilt or inconsistency. What they can challenge are two things. One is the assumption of many retributivists that the ground they are standing on is the high ground of morality (after all, utilitarians are at least more concerned with human welfare). The other is the retributivist's assumption that one must act on retributive feelings.

Notes

Introduction

1. See for example E. A. Hoebel, *The Law of Primitive Man: A Study of Comparative Legal Dynamics* (1961, Cambridge, Mass., Harvard University Press), and in particular the story of Rasmussen's Eskimo wife-stealer; also S. Roberts, *Order and Dispute: An Introduction to Legal Anthropology* (1979, Harmondsworth, Penguin).

2. Most of them were pointed out by Anthony Flew in 'The Justification of Punishment', in *Philosophy*, 3 (1954), 291ff. (reprinted in H. B. Acton (ed.), *The Philosophy of Punishment: A Collection of Papers* (1969, London, Macmillan). But the glosses are mine.

3. Modestinus (an authority quoted in Justinian's *Digest*) thought that mad criminals were 'punished enough by their madness'.

4. Directed against what Veblen called 'conspicuous consumption': the ostentatious display of affluence.

5. See Thomas Hill Green, *Works*, ed. R. L. Nettleship, 3 vols. (1883–5, London, Longmans Green).

6. See John Locke, *Second Treatise on Government* (1690, London, Churchill).

Chapter 1: Justifying sentences

1. Protagoras was a Thracian philosopher of the fifth century BC, to whom Plato attributes utilitarian views in his dialogue of that name (see e.g. C. C. W. Taylor's translation (1976, Oxford, Clarendon Press); Grotius, seventeenth-century jurist (see his *De Jure Belli et Pacis*, trans. anon. as *The Rights of War and Peace* (1738, London, Innys)); C. Beccaria, an eighteenth-century Italian noble (see e. g. his *Dei Delitti e delle Pene* (1761), trans. H. Paolucci as *On Crimes and Punishments* (1963, New York, Bobbs-Merrill)). For J. Bentham's views see his *Introduction to the Principles of Morals and Legislation* (1789, London, Payne). Mill's main contribution so far as law enforcement was concerned was his *Essay on Liberty* (1859, London, Parker). Wootton's was *Crime and the Criminal Law* (1963, London, Stevens).

2. See I. Kant, *Rechtslehre* (1796–7), trans. W. Hastie as *Philosophy of Law* (1887, Edinburgh, Clark); G. Hegel, *Philosophie des Rechts* (1854), trans. T. M. Knox as *Philosophy of Right* (1942, Oxford, Oxford University Press); F. H. Bradley, *Ethical Studies* (1876, Oxford, Clarendon Press).

3. See B. Bosanquet, *Some Suggestions in Ethics* (1918, London, Macmillan); K. G. Armstrong, 'The Retributivist Hits Back', in *Mind*, 70 (1961), 471ff.; A. Flew, 'The Justification of Punishment', in *Philosophy*, 29 (1954), 3; J. L. Mackie, 'Morality and the Retributive Emotions', in *Criminal Justice Ethics*, inaugural issue, (Winter/Spring, 1982), 3ff.; R. Nozick, *Philosophical Explanations* (1981, Oxford, Clarendon Press).

4. See N. Walker and M. Hough, *Public Attitudes to Sentencing: Surveys in Five Countries* (1988, Aldershot, Gower). Other polls have disclosed similar percentages.

5. 'The purpose of Punishment is
   to prevent activity perilous to society;
   to prevent the offender from committing criminal offences and to reform him;
   to exercise educational influence on other people in order to deter them from committing criminal offences;
   to influence development of social morals and social discipline among citizens'
   (Article 3 of the Code of 1951).

6. See A. von Hirsch, *Doing Justice: The Choice of Punishments: Report of the Committee for the Study of Incarceration* (1976, New York, Hill and Wang).

7. Examples are probation at one extreme and very long penitentiary sentences at the other.

8. Where 'just deserts' are sometimes called 'modern retributivism', as in A. J. Ashworth, *Sentencing and Penal Policy* (1983, London, Weidenfeld and Nicholson).

Chapter 2: Deterring Others

1. J. Bentham, *Introduction to the Principles of Morals and Legislation* (1789, London, Payne), was concerned with little else. It was only later that he gave much thought to designing penitentiaries so as to correct offenders.

2. For example by a former Director of the Howard League, in a letter to *The Times*.

3. Usually by writers who disapprove of it. See for example D. Beyleveld's very thorough *Bibliography on General Deterrence Research* (1980, Farnborough, Saxon House.)

4. And sometimes from intentional omissions, such as decisions not to use seat-belts. To what extent they can be induced to *think of* such precautions, thus making the omission intentional, is less certain; and we need another word for reminders of this sort.

5. Their importance is well illustrated in T. Bennett and R. Wright, *Burglars on Burglary* (1984, Aldershot, Gower).

6. There are people, however, who are attracted by the risk of death or serious injury. They may enjoy the prestige or raising of their adrenalin level. In some cases they may have what psychoanalysts have called a 'death wish', but of an ambivalent kind which makes them indulge in risky pursuits while minimizing the risk by technical or physical skill.

7. Again see Bennett and Wright, *Burglars on Burglary*.

8. See the graph in N. Walker, *Sentencing in a Rational Society* (1969, Harmondsworth, Penguin).

9. See R. G. Hood, *The Death Penalty* (1989, Oxford, Clarendon Press). The exceptions are econometric analyses of time series of homicides in the United States which suggest that executions have a beneficial effect on their incidence: but Hood is more impressed by the analyses which contradict this.

10. Conceivably, a few people may be deterred by capital punishment but not by long incarceration *and vice versa*; but if so their numbers must be more or less equal—a not very likely hypothesis.

11. Nor are we likely to know. It is not too difficult to count homicides with a high degree of accuracy, but very hard to estimate accurately how many people are involved in activities such as illicit drug-dealing.

12. If A attacks B, intending to cause him grievous bodily harm, or knowing that the attack is highly likely to do so, and as a result B dies within a year and a day, A is guilty of murder, unless he has an excuse such as self-defence, insanity, provocation, diminished responsibility, or obedience to a lawful order.

13. K. Wolpin, 'An Economic Analysis of Crime and Punishment in England and Wales, 1894–1967', in *Journal of Political Economy*, 86 (1978), 815. An econometrist specializes in statistical techniques for measuring such things as causal relationships.

14. i.e. the *higher* the imprisonment-rate the *lower* the violence-rate, and vice versa.

15. Which can be quite high—especially since the victim is often acquainted with his assailant—or quite low, as in street robberies.

16. Using 'clear-up-rates' in Britain or 'arrest-rates' in the United States. In Britain a crime is 'cleared up' if the police are satisfied that they have identified the perpetrator, even if they cannot or do not bring him to trial.

17. See Beyleveld, *Bibliography on General Deterrence Research*. Attempts have been made to argue that the direction of causation may not be *from* these variables *to* the crime-rate: for example that they may vary in response to the crime-rate, or that both kinds of variable may vary in response to other social factors. It is not possible to refute these arguments conclusively; but they are rather strained.

18. For example the ostensible clear-up-rate for shop-lifting is very high, but only because shop-liftings are not usually noticed unless the shop-lifter is caught in the act.

19. See R. M. Kimber's report, *The Effects of Wheel-Clamping in Central London* (Report no. 1156 of the Transport and Road Research Laboratory; 1984, Crowthorne).

20. See R. Baxter and C. Nuttall, 'Severe Sentences no Deterrent to Crime', in *New Society*, 31 (1975, 11ff. Judges used to cite the 'Notting Hill Gate' sentences of 1958 for racial attacks as an instance of successful exemplary sentencing, but for the reasons given in N. Walker, *Crime and Criminology* (1987, Oxford, Oxford University Press) it was a very suspect success.

Chapter 3: Educating or Satisfying Others

1. See Sollum Emlyn, preface to Cobbett, *Complete Collection of State Trials* (1730 edn., London, Payne).

2. C. Beccaria, *Dei Delitti e delle Pene* (1761).

3. See J. Fitzjames Stephen, *History of the Criminal Law of England*, ii (1883, London, Macmillan).

4. É. Durkheim, *The Division of Labour in Society* (1893), trans. G. Simpson (1965, New York, Free Press).

5. Minutes of Evidence taken before the Royal Commission on Capital Punishment, Ninth Day (1950, London, HMSO).

6. Written Evidence to the Royal Commission on the Penal System in England and Wales (1967, London, HMSO), vol. ii, part 1.

7. (1965) 51 Cr. App. Rep. 204.

8. (1974) 60 Cr. App. Rep. 74: my italics.

9. See Hastings Rashdall, *The Theory of Good and Evil*, 2 vols. (1907, Oxford, Clarendon Press).

10. See B. Bosanquet, *Some Suggestions in Ethics* (1918, London, Macmillan).

11. See A. C. Ewing, *The Morality of Punishment* (1929, London, Kegan Paul).

12. It was later reprinted in J. Feinberg, *Doing and Deserving* (1970, Princeton, NJ, Princeton University Press). What Kant really meant will be discussed in Chapter 9.

13. See Hyman Gross, *A Theory of Criminal Justice* (1979, Oxford, Clarendon Press).

14. Durkheim would probably have retorted that the cases in which offenders *are* punished are demonstrations that the law *can* act effectively, and that the fuss which is made when they *aren't* punished reminds us of the law. But in this sort of argument 'we' are law-abiding people, who do not need such demonstrations or reminders.

15. The *Daily Telegraph*, 21 June 1975.

16. For a full account of the experiment see N. Walker and M. Hough (eds.), *Public Attitudes to Sentencing: Surveys in Five Countries* (1988, Aldershot, Gower), chapter 30.

17. Ranging from 'I do not disapprove at all' to 'I disapprove strongly'.

18. See W. Moberly, *The Ethics of Punishment* (1968, London, Faber and Faber), especially pp. 212–22, and *Suffering, Innocent and Guilty* by his great-niece E. Moberly (1978, London, Society for the Propagation of Christian Knowledge), especially chapter 5. For 'eclecticism' see Chapter 15.

19. See R. A. Duff, *Trials and Punishments* (1986, Cambridge, Cambridge University Press), chapters 9, 10.

20. See the Law Commission of Canada's report, *Our Criminal Law*, (1976, Ottawa, Information Canada).

21. (1965) 51 Cr. App. Rep. 204 (my italics).

22. 269 *House of Lords Official Report* (5th series) col. 536.

23. It is true that if this became public knowledge the denunciation might well fail, whether to educate morally or to satisfy ritually: but that is simply a practical argument for actually carrying out *enough* sentences to maintain the belief that *all* are carried out.

24. For example the British Crime Surveys, and the Walker–Hough survey: see Walker and Hough (eds.), *Public Attitudes to Sentencing*, chapters 7, 10.

25. See ibid., chapter 6.

Chapter 4: Elimination and Incapacitation

1. In theory, at least. In practice, unless a prisoner behaves so violently that he is segregated, his fellow-inmates simply have to watch their step.

2. But in Louisiana, for instance, it does.

3. An 'impulsive' offender is liable to succumb to sudden temptations or provocations: a 'compulsive' one experiences desires of growing strength which he may at first resist only to succumb after a struggle, and sometimes with careful planning.

4. The Home Secretary may veto a favourable recommendation of the Board, but cannot release without a favourable one. Other systems differ in their decision-making machineries: some allot the decisive role to a judge (and his advisers). But the principles and considerations are the same.

5. Not to be confused with 'political prisoners', who have been imprisoned for non-violent, non-dishonest political activities.

6. In 1988: the percentage is likely to rise.

7. i.e. time deducted from determinate sentences for good conduct.

8. He may have formed friendships with more seasoned offenders, or learned new techniques for offending. But this danger has been exaggerated by penal reformers. His new friends or mentors are unsuccessful offenders, and their effect is likely to be that if he reoffends he will be easier to identify. For a review of the research on the harm done by incarceration see N. Walker, 'The Unwanted Effects of Long-Term Imprisonment, in A. E. Bottoms and R. Light (eds.), *Problems of Long-Term Imprisonment* (1987, Aldershot, Gower).

9. See Pauline Morris, *Prisoners and their Families* (1965, London, Allen and Unwin), and R. Shaw, *Children of Imprisoned Fathers* (1987, London, Hodder and Stoughton).

10. Most prisoners found to be mentally ill turn out to have psychiatric histories. Sometimes the first signs are observed during a custodial sentence; but they are usually symptoms of an illness such as schizophrenia which would have developed in any case, or under other sorts of stress.

11. See Dr J. Coker's letter in *British Journal of Criminology*, 23: 2 (1983), 307–8.

12. Most lifers and long-term prisoners begin their sentences in their twenties and thirties.

13. Examples are men and women who have an obsessive grudge, personal or political, against an individual or an organization.

Some prisoners even *say* that when released they will 'finish the job'.

14. P. W. Greenwood and A. Abrahamse, *Selective Incapacitation* (1982, Santa Monica, Rand).

15. The only comparable British research was designed to answer a less relevant question. What percentage of men convicted of indictable offences in 1971 would have been prevented from committing their next offence if their convictions had led to detention for a year? (The answer was 25 per cent.) But (1) most of their offences were not of the kinds from which we demand protection by long detention; (2) when we do, we have in mind periods much longer than a year. See S. Brody and R. Tarling, *Taking Offenders out of Circulation* (Home Office Research Study, 64; 1974, London, HMSO).

16. Should it, for example, include a share of the cost of hunting them down and trying them? Or, since the agencies of law-enforcement would be employed on other work if not on this, should that be excluded?

17. Such as teaching. It hardly matters whether the prohibition is pronounced by a court or—as in Britain—by the Government Department responsible for education.

18. At least so long as it does not involve the care of children: if he has been convicted of maltreating children he may find it difficult to get any kind of job involving care of the young, since employers of such staff are allowed information about his conviction.

19. As distinct from the idiosyncratic sense. Someone who knows what the individual is like may be able to say that the experience of offending (or its consequences) has rendered him *less* likely to offend than the man with a clean record. But if all that we know is that he has offended the statistics tell us that he is *more* likely. And this is true whether we are talking about offences in general or specific kinds of offences.

20. See W. C. Kvaraceus, *Anxious Youth* (1966, Columbus, Ohio).

Chapter 5: Correction

1. Although 'labelling theory' argued that it is likely to have the opposite effect, either by altering his self-image for the worse or by making him feel that the only people who would accept him as a friend would be those who had similar reputations, and would thus reinforce his delinquent values. Undoubtedly stigma can have such

effects. The point I am making here is merely that it may sometimes be beneficial.

2. A term sometimes used loosely nowadays to mean 'reform', especially in the United States, where the evil reputation of 'reformatories' for the young led to the disuse of the word.

3. See E. Powers and H. Witmer, *An Experiment in the Prevention of Delinquency: The Cambridge–Somerville Youth Study* (1951, New York, Columbia University Press).

4. Or even had been detected in doing so but had not been the subject of official action because of the intervention of well-meaning social workers (as is said to have been revealed in at least one Californian study of parole).

5. When randomization has been achieved it has usually been managed administratively. For example, in the English 'pooled borstal allocation experiment', youths sentenced to borstal training were randomly selected to be sent to borstals with very different regimes, one based on traditional discipline, one on group counselling, one on 'case-work' which studied the family and social circumstances in which they had offended, and tried to find remedies. Only the case-work regime had better results. See Mark Williams, *A Study of Some Aspects of Borstal Allocation* (Report No. 33 of the Prison Department Psychologists; 1970, unpublished).

6. See for example N. Walker, *Sentencing: Theory, Law and Practice* (1985, London, Butterworths), chapter 6.

7. The comparison allowed for type of offence, previous convictions and the time for which actual imprisonment put offenders out of action. (Since they were all over 21 it was not necessary to allow for age: it made a very small difference to reconviction probabilities.) An exception to the finding was men with five or more previous convictions: their reconviction-rate was so high (88 per cent) that nine out of ten were clearly bound to be reconvicted whatever was done to them.

8. See D. Ward, *Validity of the Reconviction Prediction Score* (Home Office Research Study, 94; 1987, London, HMSO), chapter 5.

9. It may be wondered how, if aggregate statistics show no differences, there can be cases in which individuals have benefited. The answer is probably that some other individuals become *more* likely to be reconvicted, perhaps because they are encouraged by what they regard as a 'let-off'.

10. The traditional slogan of the probation service.

11. Intensification consisted not only of more frequent appointments but also of closer attention to factors, such as delinquent associates, which seemed to contribute to their misbehaviour. See M. S. Folkard *et al.*, *IMPACT* ii (Home Office Research Study 36; 1976, London, HMSO).

12. Especially by official publications such as *The Sentence of the Court* (1986 edn., Home Office, London, HMSO), which ridiculously exaggerates the effectiveness of probation orders.

13. Robert Martinson, 'What Works?', in *Public Interest*, 35 (1974).

14. See for example R. G. Hood and R. Sparks, *Key Issues in Criminology* (1970, London, Weidenfeld and Nicholson).

15. Robert Martinson, 'New Findings, New Views: A Note of Caution regarding Sentencing Reform', in *Hofstra Law Review*, 7: 2 (1979), 243 ff.

16. See S. Adams, 'The Pico Project', in N. Johnston *et al.* (eds.), *The Sociology of Punishment and Corrections* (1962, London, Wiley), 213 ff.

17. See J. Braithwaite, *Crime, Shame and Reintegration* (1989, Cambridge, Cambridge University Press).

Chapter 6: Human Sacrifice?

1. See I. Kant, *Rechtslehre* (1796–7), trans. W. Hastie as *Philosophy of Law* (1887, Edinburgh, Clark). The italics are mine, but it is worth noting that wherever he talks of using people 'as a means' he qualifies it in this way.

2. A fraction often used in the argument.

3. In theory, of course, a 'do-they-again?' follow-up should extend to the grave; but the probability of recidivism declines with each year of law-abiding liberty. When a man or woman has clearly refrained from serious violence for five or six years the likelihood that they will commit it again has become small enough to be disregarded for statistical purposes. There are exceptions, among whom are people who are subject to episodes of schizophrenia or depression, or who respond to stress by heavy drinking which culminates in violence. Supervisors and associates, however, can usually notice the warning signs.

4. See for example N. Walker, *Sentencing: Theory, Law and Practice* (1985, London, Butterworths), 370.

5. See *A New Penal System*: English summary of a report by the

Working Group for Criminal Policy of the National Swedish Council for Crime Prevention (1978, Stockholm).

6. See J. Floud and W. Young, *Dangerousness and Criminal Justice*, (1981, London, Heinemann).

7. Of course the police keep a closer eye on football fans and other groups of young men who seem likely to behave violently; and some individuals enjoy police protection. But this hardly contradicts the argument about the application of *sentences*.

8. Although they may make threats, weapon-carrying, and such-like, grounds for convicting them.

Chapter 7: The Sacrosanct Personality

1. It was originally published in *Res Judicatae: The Journal of the Law Students' Society, Victoria* (Australia), 6 (1953), 2. It is a pity that Lewis used the adjective 'humanitarian', since what he was attacking was not what genuine humanitarians advocate: see Chapter 16.

2. Nowadays known as the 'mentally handicapped' or (in the English Mental Health Act of 1983) 'mentally impaired'. Every modern generation seems to need a new euphemism for them: 'idiots', 'mental defectives', 'the mentally subnormal', or even—the supreme euphemism of American educationalists—'exceptional'. Lewis, by the way, may well have meant to include the mentally ill, or at least severe and chronic examples, but he does not say so.

3. Yet of course the strict disciplinary regimes of many custodial establishments did result in temporary or even permanent conditioning, for example in obedience to authority, even if they were not based on psychologists' findings as regards reinforcing or aversive stimuli.

4. 'Laboratory' is another example of C. S. Lewis's rhetoric. The Viennese psychoanalysts had no laboratories, and would have considered them useless.

5. N. Kittrie, *The Right to be Different* (1971, Baltimore, The Johns Hopkins Press).

6. See J. S. Mill, *On Liberty* (1859, London, Parker).

7. See for example J. Feinberg, 'The Child's Right to an Open Future', in A. I. Melden (ed.), *Human Rights* (Belmont, Calif., Wadsworth).

Chapter 8: Blaming and Excusing?

1. See for example J. G. Cottingham, 'Varieties of Retribution', *Philosophical Quarterly*, 29 (1979), 238ff.

2. From the Latin word *talis*, which means 'of the same kind'. Some talionic codes went as far as to prescribe talionic penalties for false accusers, so that those whose accusations were not upheld suffered the fate which the accused person would have suffered: a rule enjoined for example by Deuteronomy 19: 19.

3. Strictly speaking I should add 'or omissions' whenever I mention 'acts' or 'actions'; but that would be unnecessarily tedious.

4. David Hume argued this in the eighteenth century (in his *Inquiry concerning Human Understanding* (Edinburgh, Clark), chapter VIII, paragraph 2). John Rawls, *Theory of Justice* (1973, Oxford, Oxford University Press) takes it for granted. George Fletcher developed the point more thoroughly in *Rethinking Criminal Law* (1978, Boston, Mass., Little, Brown). Andrew von Hirsch used it to argue the relevance of previous convictions to severity of sentences in *Past or Future Crimes* (1985, Manchester, Manchester University Press).

Chapter 9: Justifying Retribution

1. See for example Michael S. Moore, 'The Moral Worth of Retribution', in F. Schoeman (ed.), *Responsibility, Character and the Emotions* (1987, Cambridge, Cambridge University Press).

2. True, in early stages of most societies' penal development, compensation is usually accepted as a way of 'settling' wrongs done by individuals to each other. But it usually ceases to be completely acceptable when crimes that 'breach the peace' are distinguished from mere civil wrongs.

3. See B. Bosanquet, *Some Suggestions in Ethics* (1918, London, Macmillan).

4. By David Cooper, 'Hegel's Theory of Punishment', in Z. A. Pelczynski (ed.), *Hegel's Political Philosophy: Problems and Perspectives* (1971, Cambridge, Cambridge University Press).

5. See for example Herbert Morris, 'Persons and Punishment', in *Monist*, 52 (1968), 475ff.; J. G. Murphy, *Retribution, Justice and Therapy* (1979, Dordrecht, Holland, Reidel), part 2; A. von Hirsch, *Doing Justice: The Choice of Punishments. Report of the Committee for the Study of Incarceration* (1976, New York, Hill and Wang). It is worth noting, however, that Morris later

preferred 'A Paternalistic Theory of Punishment', in *American Philosophical Quarterly*, 18: 4 (1981), 263ff., and that von Hirsch later preferred a symbolic justification in *Past or Future Crimes* (1985, Manchester, Manchester University Press) as we shall see later in this chapter.

6. See R. A. Duff, *Trials and Punishments* (1986, Cambridge, Cambridge University Press).

7. The *locus classicus* for his views on this subject is the short section on 'The Right of Punishing' in I. Kant, *Rechtslehre* (1796–7), trans. W. Hastie as *Philosophy of Law* (1887, Edinburgh, Clark). But for his explanations of 'categorical imperatives' see his *Grundlegung zur Metaphysik der Sitten* (1785), trans. T. K. Abbott as *Fundamental Principles of the Metaphysic of Morals* (1883, London, Longmans Green).

8. John Cottingham, 'Varieties of Retribution', in *Philosophical Quarterly*, 29 (1979), 238ff., interprets this as 'placation theory': if the last murderer is not executed God will be angry. Certainly 'blood-guilt' (*Blutschuld*) sounds superstitious; but Kant does not mention God. It seems more likely that he meant what he said: that those who could but don't execute the last murderer are to some extent guilty of his bloodshed.

9. We are entitled for the sake of argument to assume that this would be feasible.

10. For a recent example see E. Moberly, *Suffering, Innocent and Guilty* (1978, London, Society for the Propagation of Christian Knowledge).

11. In the Convocation of York on 15 May 1962.

12. See F. H. Bradley, *Ethical Studies* (1876, Oxford, Clarendon Press).

13. Von Hirsch, *Past or Future Crimes*.

14. See Duff, *Trials and Punishments*. Duff adopts an unusual convention and consistently refers to the criminal as feminine.

15. Was Nozick echoing Morgan Forster's famous exhortation?

16. Nozick's synonym for 'utilitarian'.

Chapter 10: A Rule-explanation?

1. The idea was suggested to me by reading the appendix to W. D. Ross, *The Right and the Good* (1930, Oxford, Clarendon Press), where he says that in punishing offenders the State is keeping a promise. More recently, after outlining my suggestion in *Crime*

and Criminology (1987, Oxford, Oxford University Press), I noticed that J. D. Mabbott, in an article first published in 1939, came close to the idea; but he did not have the advantage of post-war studies of human rule-following. (His article can be found in H. B. Acton (ed.), *The Philosophy of Punishment: A Collection of Papers* (1969, London, Macmillan).)

2. See H. Garfinkel, *Studies in Ethnomethodology* (1967, Englewood Cliffs, NJ, Prentice-Hall). Another illuminating book about rule-following is R. Harré and P. Secord, *The Explanation of Social Behaviour* (1972, Oxford, Blackwell).

3. See for example L. Berkowitz and R. Geen, 'Film Violence and the Cue Properties of Available Targets', in *Journal of Personality and Social Psychology*, 3, (1966), 525ff. And G. Sykes and D. Matza describe vividly how delinquents 'neutralize' feelings of guilt about personal violence, in 'Techniques of Neutralization', in *American Sociological Review*, 22 (1959), 664ff.

4. A rule which merely offers the sentencer a choice between penalties is still prescriptive, if he must choose one of them, whereas one which allows him to let the offender off any penalty is permissive.

5. More precisely, as David Thomas points out in *Principles of Sentencing* (1970, London, Heinemann), they have in mind a 'normal range' where the length of prison sentences is concerned. This allows some latitude for mitigating or aggravating considerations.

6. Or if he wants simply to 'experiment' in order to see whether one measure is more effective than another.

7. H. L. A. Hart, *Punishment and Responsibility* (1968, Oxford, Clarendon Press).

Chapter 11: The Negative Principle

1. Whether it is a rule or a principle (to adopt Dworkin's distinction) is a question which for the moment hardly matters. Principles, according to Dworkin, are imprecise guide-lines which admit exceptions, and are usually interpreted by rules that say when they apply and how to apply them. See R. Dworkin, *Taking Rights Seriously* (1977, London, Duckworth). In this case the principle might be 'no penalty without desert', and the 'negative rules', to use my phrase, would be interpretations of this principle.

2. As Sergeant Boshears claimed to have done in 1963: see N. Walker, *Crime and Insanity in England*, i (1968, Edinburgh Edinburgh University Press).

3. Examples are the handling of under-age delinquents by 'welfare' or 'family' courts, and the committal of 'insane' offenders by civil, not criminal courts (although in most Commonwealth countries it is still the criminal court which commits.)

4. See H. L. A. Hart, *Punishment and Responsibility* (1968, Oxford, Clarendon Press).

5. See J. Rawls, *A Theory of Justice* (1973, Oxford, Oxford University Press). I hope that I have not oversimplified the central point of this massive and closely argued book.

6. Such a rule would not afford young children as much protection against being penalized as they enjoy at present; but I have pointed out (in N. Walker, *Crime and Criminology* (1987, Oxford, Oxford University Press)) that it makes more sense to exempt them from certain kinds of penalty than to exempt them from all liability.

Chapter 12: Commensurability and Proportionality

1. See T. Sellin and M. Wolfgang, *The Measurement of Delinquency* (1964, New York, Wiley), and P. Rossi *et al.*, 'The Seriousness of Crime: Normative Structure and Individual Differences', in *American Journal of Sociology*, 39, (1974), 224ff. (which used a better sample).

2. Previous convictions of a different kind are either obviously relevant (as when a fraudster has a record of cheque-bouncing) or obviously irrelevant (as when his record is limited to bad driving).

3. J. Bentham, *Introduction to the Principles of Morals and of Legislation* (1789, London, Payne).

4. It is remarkable how few philosophers or jurists acknowledged Bentham's point. The Victorian philosopher Thomas Hill Green did, but dismissed it summarily: 'It is not in the power of the state to regulate the amount of pain which it causes to the person whom it punishes' ('The Right of the State to Punish', in Thomas Hill Green, *Works*, ed. R. Nettleship, ii (1885, London, Longmans Green).

5. For examples see David Thomas, *Current Sentencing Practice* (1982, London, Sweet and Maxwell) a loose-leaf reference book with many supplements which is officially supplied to judges who try criminal cases.

6. A supernatural functionary known to most religions of Near-Eastern origin. His duty is to record the good and evil deeds of

men and report them when they come to final judgment. Since he does not determine their fate his reports must be more like balance-sheets than price-lists.

7. Hegel, *Philosophie des Rechts* (1854), trans. T. M. Knox as *Philosophy of Right* (1942, Oxford, Oxford University Press). Hegel was not the first to make this point. Portia does so in *The Merchant of Venice* when rebutting Shylock's claim for a pound of flesh. Nor was Shakespeare being original: he probably got the idea from a sixteenth-century Italian play, *Il Pecorone*; or even from the thirteenth-century *Gesta Romanorum*. (I owe this information to Dr Paul Hammond.)

8. From A. R. N. Cross, *The English Sentencing System* (1971; 2nd edn., 1975, London, Butterworths).

9. See C. Beccaria, *Dei Delitti e delle Pene* (1761).

10. See Bentham, *Introduction to the Principles of Morals and of Legislation*.

11. See for example C. L. Ten, *Crime, Guilt and Punishment* (1981, Oxford, Clarendon Press).

12. For example see David Thomas's monthly commentaries on sentencing decisions of the Court of Appeal in the *Criminal Law Review* (1971–).

13. See for instance the reasoning of the Court of Appeal in *R.*v. *Lowe* (Times Law Reports, 14 November 1989).

14. See for instance *R.* v. *Reeves* (*Criminal Law Review*, 67 (1964)). He and another man had dishonestly received twenty stolen pitch-fibre pipes. The other man wisely chose trial by magistrates, and was fined £25. Reeves chose trial by jury, and was sentenced to nine months' imprisonment. When he appealed, the Court of Criminal Appeal did not consider this excessive. On the contrary they said his accomplice's sentence was too lenient. Yet they felt obliged to reduce Reeve's sentence so as to secure his immediate release.

Chapter 13: Unintended Punishment

1. Exceptions are Pauline Morris, *Prisoners and their Families* (1965, London, Allen and Unwin), and R. Shaw, *Children of Imprisoned Fathers* (1987, London, Hodder and Stoughton).

2. I owe this information to Professor Alberto Cadoppi of the University of Trento.

3. For reviews of the evidence see D. P. Farrington's two articles 'The Effects of Public Labelling', in *British Journal of Criminology*, 17: 2 (1977), 112ff., and (with others), 'The Persistence of Labelling Effects', in *British Journal of Criminology* 18: 3 (1978), 227ff. More sceptical is C. Tittle, 'Labelling and Crime: An Evaluation', in W. Gove (ed.), *The Labelling of Deviance* (1980, London, Sage).

4. See J. P. Martin and D. Webster, *The Social Consequences of Conviction* (1971, London, Heinemann).

5. For a discussion of the British Rehabilitation of Offenders Act 1974 and other systems see N. Walker, *Punishment, Danger and Stigma* (1980, Oxford, Blackwell).

6. Occasionally a judge expressly lightens a sentence because the offender has lost a well-paid position of trust and is unlikely to get another. But there has been no attempt to formulate a rule which enjoins this.

Chapter 14: Repentance, Reparation, Forgiveness, and Mercy

1. For a subtle and interesting book by two philosophers see J. G. Murphy and J. Hampton, *Forgiveness and Mercy* (1988, Cambridge, Cambridge University Press).

2. A policy approved by the English Court of Appeal, in order to save courts' time by discouraging 'not guilty' pleas.

3. 'Reparation' is nowadays a generic term, denoting not only financial compensation but also 'restitution' (the return of property to its rightful owner) and the repair of criminal damage. What offenders usually offer, and what courts usually order, is financial compensation; and this is what I have therefore used in my examples.

4. Notably by Murphy, in Murphy and Hampton, *Forgiveness and Mercy*, chapter 1.

5. See ibid., chapter 2.

6. See A. Smart's article on 'Mercy', in H. B. Acton (ed.) *The Philosophy of Punishment: A Collection of Papers* (1969, London, Macmillan).

7. See Murphy and Hampton, *Forgiveness and Mercy*, chapter 4.

8. Ibid, chapter 5.

9. An exception was the British rule that it should be used in capital cases when there was 'a scintilla of doubt' about the guilt of the

condemned man. This would occasionally happen in spite of judges' strict instructions to jurors that they must be sure of his guilt 'beyond reasonable doubt'. In Scotland, where a jury could convict by a majority of 8 to 7, this principle was an important one.

Chapter 15: Jigsaw, Eclectic, and Hybrid Compromises

1. See H. L. A. Hart, *Punishment and Responsibility* (1968, Oxford, Clarendon Press), chapter 1. He is not, however, explicit as to what should determine the severity of unmitigated punishment: I cannot find in this chapter all the views attributed to him by C. L. Ten in his *Crime, Guilt and Punishment* (1987, Oxford, Clarendon Press).

2. See Ten, *Crime, Guilt and Punishment*.

3. Why must the suffering be 'much' less, and not merely less?

4. This shows how hard it is to devise a 'thought-experiment' of this kind. It is arguable that disclosing his existence and then punishing him would (1) create a demand and satisfy it; (2) deter potential imitators by impressing them with the difficulty of eluding justice. But for the sake of argument we must ignore points of this sort.

5. See Liddell and Scott, *Greek–English Lexicon* (1897 and later edns., Oxford, Clarendon Press).

6. From David Thomas, *Principles of Sentencing in the Court of Appeal* (1970; 1979 edn., London, Heinemann). When this passage was first published in 1970, it was not so much a description as a rationalization: few sentencers thought so clearly. Read as a description, however, it was very persuasive, and within a few years had become a fair account of the way in which many—even most—judges claimed to reason.

7. When originally coined by Wahlberg in 1869 in *Das Prinzip der Individualisierung in der Strafrechtspflege*, the term did not imply a utilitarian approach, being used merely to connote the mitigation or aggravation of punishment in the light of the circumstances of the case (see R. Salleilles, *L'Individualisation de la peine* (3rd edn., 1927, Paris, Presses Universitaire de France), trans. R. S. Jastrow as *The Individualisation of Punishment* (1911, London, Heinemann). But Ruggles-Brise, the English prison administrator, used it in an eclectic sense when talking about the Borstal system; and this is how it is used by Thomas.

8. In my seminars with magistrates I have been made to realize that some do not distinguish between retribution and deterrence. This makes eclecticism all the easier!

9. For a discussion of this problem see Paul H. Robinson, 'Hybrid Principles for the Distribution of Criminal Sanctions', in *Northwestern University Law Review*, 82: 1 (1988) 19ff., and N. Walker, *Sentencing: Theory, Law and Practice* (1986, London, Butterworths), chapter 8. Neither, however, deals with all the possibilities.

10. England replaced the distinction in 1967, and replaced it with one between 'arrestable' and 'non-arrestable' offences.

11. See *Report of the Victorian Sentencing Committee* (1988, Melbourne, the Victorian Attorney-General's Department), iii. 24. I am grateful to David Thomas for drawing my attention to it.

12. The Supreme Court of Victoria may say that this is not what they meant. But I have taken their proposal at its face value because it illustrates a rule that deserves serious consideration.

13. See Robinson, 'Hybrid Principles for the Distribution of Criminal Sanctions'. I hope he will forgive me for expressing his rule in terms that will be clearer to English readers, and for my glosses on it.

14. See F. Pakenham (Lord Longford), *The Idea of Punishment* (1961, London, Chapman), and Norval Morris, *Madness and the Criminal Law* (1982, Chicago, Ill., Chicago University Press). Morris's treatment is more thorough than Longford's.

15. A few penalties are mandatory: life for murder, death for treason, disqualification for serious traffic offences. And for quite a number of serious crimes 'life' is a permissible sentence, although the English Court of Appeal tends to confine it to offenders whose mental instability makes them dangerous.

16. When it is used as a *lower* limit it can still be regarded as obligatory.

17. A limiting retributivist who relies on a superstitious explanation would have to believe in a Jehovah who had been influenced by Bentham.

Chapter 16: Humanitarian Limits

1. See R. Fitzgerald and P. C. Ellsworth, 'Due Process vs. Crime Control: Death Qualification and Jury Attitudes', in *Law and Human Behaviour*, 8 (1984), 31ff.

2. For example, the forty-two-year sentence imposed on George Blake, who betrayed many British agents to the Soviets, seemed so excessive to two compatriots that they encouraged and helped him

to escape, in spite of their strong moral disapproval of his treachery.

3. See H. C. Baldry, *The Unity of Mankind in Greek Thought* (1965, Cambridge, Cambridge University Press).

4. See W. H. Lecky, *History of European Morals from Augustus to Charlemagne* (1877, London, Longmans Green). The few psychologists (most of them in the United States) who have interested themselves in humanitarian attitudes have not found them to be associated with 'religiosity': if anything the reverse. See for instance J. De Fronzo, 'Religion and Humanitarianism in Eysenck's T-Dimension and Left–Right Political Orientation', in *Journal of Personality and Social Psychology*, 21: 3 (1972), 265ff.

5. N. Christie, *Limits to Pain* (1981, Oxford, Martin Robertson).

6. See the seventeenth-century English Bill of Rights and the United States' Constitution.

7. See the United Nations, *Universal Declaration of Human Rights* (1948, New York), and *The European Convention on Human Rights*, (1952, Strasbourg), especially Article 3.

8. So far the only form of punishment which has been judicially declared 'inhuman' within the meaning of the *European Convention on Human Rights* is the Greek practice of beating the feet (see Sir James Fawcett, *The Application of the European Convention on Human Rights* (1969; 1987 edn., Oxford, Clarendon Press). As for 'degradation', its meaning has not yet been made clearer by judicial decisions. In 1989 in the case of *Jens Soering* the European Court of Human Rights decided that prolonged *delays* in carrying out the death sentence constituted inhuman or degrading treatment, and refused to approve his extradition to the United States for this reason; but they did not condemn capital punishment itself.

9. The United States' Constitution adds 'unusual', but it is hard to see why merely being unusual should rule out any form of punishment; and there does not seem to be any case in which the United States Supreme Court has relied on this word to declare any form of penalty unconstitutional (see H. Bedau, *Death is Different* (1987, Boston, Mass., North-Eastern University Press)). Perhaps what the original draftsmen meant was not merely 'unusual' but 'uncustomary'. In the seventeenth century Continental judges would sometimes invent novel penalties, not provided for by law or custom, and thus not taken into account as a possibility by the offender. (Even twentieth-century United States' judges are not above inventiveness. In 1978 a Californian judge ordered a cannabis-grower to parade one of his forbidden plants in front of

the court-house on Sundays, wearing a placard declaring his crime.)

10. As Ronald Dworkin points out in *Taking Rights Seriously* (1977, London, Duckworth).

Chapter 17: Why Compromise?

1. See Chapter 3.

2. For example by concealing the difference between the declared length of a prison sentence and the time actually served.

The Argument

1. See F. Nietzsche, *Zur Genealogie der Moral* (1887), trans. W. Kaufmann as *The Genealogy of Morals* (1967, New York, Random House).

Further Reading

Anthropology of Law Enforcement

E. A. Hoebel, *The Law of Primitive Man: A Study of Comparative Legal Dynamics* (1961, Cambridge, Mass., Harvard University Press) (for primitive solutions).

A. Phillips, *Ancient Israel's Criminal Law* (1970, Oxford, Blackwell) (more specialized).

S. Roberts, *Order and Dispute: An Introduction to Legal Anthropology* (1979 Harmondsworth, Penguin) (more theoretical).

Blaming and Forgiving

J. G. Murphy and J. Hampton, *Forgiveness and Mercy* (1988, Cambridge, Cambridge University Press) (a good dialogue).

F. Schoeman (ed.), *Responsibility, Character and the Emotions* (1987, Cambridge, Cambridge University Press) (some subtle essays).

Correcting Offenders

S. R. Brody, *The Effectiveness of Sentencing: A Review of the Literature* (Home Office Research Study, 35; 1976, London, HMSO) (readable).

D. Lipton, R. Martinson, and J. Wilks, *The Effectiveness of Correctional Treatment: A Survey of Treatment Evaluation Studies* (1975, New York, Praeger) (a work of reference, with summaries of methods and findings).

J. Q. Wilson, '"What Works?" Revisited', in *Public Interest* (1986) (more optimistic).

Desert

H. B. Acton (ed.), *The Philosophy of Punishment: A Collection of Papers* (1969, London, Macmillan) (most of the contributors were retributivists).

A. von Hirsch, *Doing Justice: The Choice of Punishments: Report of the Committee for the Study of Incarceration* (1976, New York, Hill and Wang) (the original manifesto of 'just deserters').

E. Moberly, *Suffering, Innocent and Guilty* (1978, London, Society for the Propagation of Christian Knowledge) (one theologian's viewpoint).

Deterrence

J. Andenaes, *Punishment and Deterrence* (1974, Ann Arbor, Mich., University of Michigan Press) (for a non-scientific, common-sense approach).

D. Beyleveld, *A Bibliography on General Deterrence Research* (1980, Farnborough, Saxon House) (a massive and complex reference book, with summaries of methods and findings).

J. F. Gibbs, *Crime, Punishment and Deterrence* (1975, Amsterdam, Elsevier).

F. E. Zimring and G. Hawkins, *Deterrence: The Legal Threat in Crime Control* (1973, Chicago, Ill., Chicago University Press).

Eclecticism

W. Moberly, *The Ethics of Punishment* (1968, London, Faber and Faber) (an example of exuberant eclecticism, but not a discussion of it, which is hard to find).

Educating the Public

N. Walker and M. Hough, *Public Attitudes to Sentencing: Surveys in Five Countries* (1988, Aldershot, Gower) (especially chapters 3, 6, 10).

Elimination

H. Bedau, *Death is Different* (1987, Boston, Mass., North-Eastern University Press) (especially for the United States' legal thinking).

K. C. Haas and J. A. Inciardi (eds.), *Challenging Capital Punishment* (1988, London, Sage) (for arguments and recent findings).

Humanity

L. C. Berkson, *The Concept of Cruel and Unusual Punishment* (1975, Lexington, Heath) (not quite up to date now, but still a good overview of the United States' 'constitutional' approach).

N. Christie, *Limits to Pain* (1981, Oxford, Martin Robertson) (without much theory).

Encyclopaedia Britannica (15th edn., 1985), article on 'Humanitarianism' (an excellent short history, though not now quite up to date).

Incapacitation

J. Floud and W. Young, *Dangerousness and Criminal Justice* (1981, London, Heinemann) (the report of a very thorough committee).

A. von Hirsch, *Past or Future Crimes* (1985, Manchester, Manchester University Press) (more sophisticated than his *Doing Justice*).

L. Sleffel, *The Law and the Dangerous Criminal: Statutory Attempts at Definition and Control* (1977, Lexington, Heath) (about United States' statutes).

Justifying Punishment

H. B. Acton (ed.), *The Philosophy of Punishment: A Collection of Papers* (1969, London, Macmillan) (some quibbling, some squabbling mostly by retributivists).

R. A. Duff, *Trials and Punishments* (1986, Cambridge, Cambridge University Press) (for the penitential approach).

H. Gross, *A Theory of Criminal Justice* (1979, Oxford, Clarendon Press) (for a Benthamite's 'anti-impunity theory').

H. L. A. Hart, *Punishment and Responsibility* (1968, Oxford, Clarendon Press) (a modern classic).

T. Honderich, *Punishment: The Supposed Justifications* (1969; rev. edn., 1976, Harmondsworth, Penguin) (up-to-date philosophy, not so up-to-date penology).

C. L. Ten, *Crime, Guilt and Punishment* (1987, Oxford, Clarendon Press) (for the amphibian way).

Sentencing

A. J. Ashworth, *Sentencing and Penal Policy* (1983, London, Weidenfeld and Nicholson) (informative about ways in which English judges reason).

K. Pease and M. Wasik *Sentencing Reform: Guidance or Guidelines?* (1987, Manchester, Manchester University Press) (especially the chapters about guideline sentencing in the United States).

D. A. Thomas, *Principles of Sentencing in the Court of Appeal* (1979, London, Heinemann) (still a classic).

N. Walker, *Sentencing: Theory, Law and Practice* (1986, London, Butterworths) (contrasts theory with what sentences mean in practice).

Utility

C. Beccaria, *Dei Delitti e delle Pene* (1761), trans. anon. as *An Essay on Crimes and Punishments* (1764, London, Newbery), trans. H. Paolucci as *On Crimes and Punishments* (1963, New York, Bobbs-Merrill). (The original manifesto of utilitarian thinking about penalties.)

J. Bentham, *Introduction to the Principles of Morals and of Legislation* (1798, London, Payne) (the utilitarian bible of minimum deterrence).

N. Walker, *Punishment, Danger and Stigma* (1980, Oxford, Blackwell) (for some aspects of utility).

B. Wootton, *Crime and the Criminal Law* (1963, London, Stevens) (utilitarianism carried rather far).

Index

Italic numbers refer to the Notes and Further Reading

OXFORD

MORE OXFORD PAPERBACKS

Details of a selection of other Oxford Paperbacks follow. A complete list of Oxford Paperbacks, including The World's Classics, Twentieth-Century Classics, OPUS, Past Masters, Oxford Authors, Oxford Shakespeare, and Oxford Paperback Reference, is available in the UK from the General Publicity Department, Oxford University Press (RS), Walton Street, Oxford, OX2 6DP.

In the USA, complete lists are available from the Paperbacks Marketing Manager, Oxford University Press, 200 Madison Avenue, New York, NY 10016.

Oxford Paperbacks are available from all good bookshops. In case of difficulty, customers in the UK can order direct from Oxford University Press Bookshop, 116 High Street, Oxford, Freepost, OX1 4BR, enclosing full payment. Please add 10 per cent of the published price for postage and packing.

POLITICS IN OXFORD PAPERBACKS

Oxford Paperbacks offers incisive and provocative studies of the political ideologies and institutions that have shaped the modern world since 1945.

GOD SAVE ULSTER!

The Religion and Politics of Paisleyism

Steve Bruce

Ian Paisley in the only modern Western leader to have founded his own Church and political party, and his enduring popularity and success mirror the complicated issues which continue to plague Northern Ireland. This book is the first serious analysis of his religious and political careers and a unique insight into Unionist politics and religion in Northern Ireland today.

Since it was founded in 1951, the Free Presbyterian Church of Ulster has grown steadily; it now comprises some 14,000 members in fifty congregations in Ulster and ten branches overseas. The Democratic Unionist Party, formed in 1971, now speaks for about half of the Unionist voters in Northern Ireland, and the personal standing of the man who leads both these movements was confirmed in 1979 when Ian R. K. Paisley received more votes than any other member of the European Parliament. While not neglecting Paisley's 'charismatic' qualities, Steve Bruce argues that the key to his success has been his ability to embody and represent traditional evangelical Protantism and traditional Ulster Unionism.

'original and profound . . . I cannot praise this book too highly.'
Bernard Crick, *New Society*

Also in Oxford Paperbacks:

Freedom Under Thatcher Keith Ewing and Conor Gearty
Strong Leadership Graham Little
The Thatcher Effect Dennis Kavanagh and Anthony Seldon

RELIGION AND THEOLOGY
IN OXFORD PAPERBACKS

Oxford Paperbacks offers incisive studies of the philosophies and ceremonies of the world's major religions, including Christianity, Judaism, Islam, Buddhism, and Hinduism.

A HISTORY OF HERESY

David Christie-Murray

'Heresy, a cynic might say, is the opinion held by a minority of men which the majority declares unacceptable and is strong enough to punish.'

What is heresy? Who were the great heretics and what did they believe? Why might those originally condemned as heretics come to be regarded as martyrs and cherished as saints?

Heretics, those who dissent from orthodox Christian belief, have existed at all times since the Christian Church was founded and the first Christians became themselves heretics within Judaism. From earliest times too, politics, orthodoxy, and heresy have been inextricably entwined—to be a heretic was often to be a traitor and punishable by death at the stake—and heresy deserves to be placed against the background of political and social developments which shaped it.

This book is a vivid combination of narrative and comment which succeeds in both re-creating historical events and elucidating the most important—and most disputed—doctrines and philosophies.

Also in Oxford Paperbacks:

Christianity in the West 1400–1700   John Bossy
John Henry Newman: A Biography   Ian Ker
Islam: The Straight Path   John L. Esposito

HISTORY IN OXFORD PAPERBACKS

Oxford Paperbacks' superb history list offers books on a wide range of topics from ancient to modern times, whether general period studies or assessments of particular events, movements, or personalities.

THE STRUGGLE FOR
THE MASTERY OF EUROPE 1848–1918

A. J. P. Taylor

The fall of Metternich in the revolutions of 1848 heralded an era of unprecedented nationalism in Europe, culminating in the collapse of the Hapsburg, Romanov, and Hohenzollern dynasties at the end of the First World War. In the intervening seventy years the boundaries of Europe changed dramatically from those established at Vienna in 1815. Cavour championed the cause of *Risorgimento* in Italy; Bismarck's three wars brought about the unification of Germany; Serbia and Bulgaria gained their independence courtesy of the decline of Turkey—'the sick man of Europe'; while the great powers scrambled for places in the sun in Africa. However, with America's entry into the war and President Wilson's adherence to idealistic internationalist principles, Europe ceased to be the centre of the world, although its problems, still primarily revolving around nationalist aspirations, were to smash the Treaty of Versailles and plunge the world into war once more.

A. J. P. Taylor has drawn the material for his account of this turbulent period from the many volumes of diplomatic documents which have been published in the five major European languages. By using vivid language and forceful characterization, he has produced a book that is as much a work of literature as a contribution to scientific history.

'One of the glories of twentieth-century writing.' *Observer*

Also in Oxford Paperbacks:

Portrait of an Age: Victorian England   G. M. Young
Germany 1866–1945   Gorden A. Craig
The Russian Revolution 1917–1932   Sheila Fitzpatrick
France 1848–1945   Theodore Zeldin

HISTORY IN OXFORD PAPERBACKS

Oxford Paperbacks offers a comprehensive list of books on British history, ranging from Frank Stenton's *Anglo-Saxon England* to John Guy's *Tudor England*, and from Christopher Hill's *A Turbulent, Seditious, and Factious People* to Kenneth O. Morgan's *Labour in Power: 1945–1951*.

TUDOR ENGLAND

John Guy

Tudor England is a compelling account of political and religious developments from the advent of the Tudors in the 1460s to the death of Elizabeth I in 1603.

Following Henry VII's capture of the Crown at Bosworth in 1485, Tudor England witnessed far-reaching changes in government and the Reformation of the Church under Henry VIII, Edward VI, Mary, and Elizabeth; that story is enriched here with character studies of the monarchs and politicians that bring to life their personalities as well as their policies.

Authoritative, clearly argued, and crisply written, this comprehensive book will be indispensable to anyone interested in the Tudor Age.

'lucid, scholarly, remarkably accomplished . . . an excellent overview' *Sunday Times*

'the first comprehensive history of Tudor England for more than thirty years' Patrick Collinson, *Observer*

Also in Oxford Paperbacks:

John Calvin   William J. Bouwsma
Early Modern France 1515–1715   Robin Briggs
The Spanish Armada   Felipe Fernández-Armesto
Time in History   G. J. Whitrow

KIERKEGAARD

Patrick Gardiner

Søren Kierkegaard (1813–55), one of the most original thinkers
of the nineteenth century, wrote widely on religious,
philosophical, and literary themes. But his idiosyncratic manner of presenting some of his leading ideas initially obscured
their fundamental import.

This book shows how Kierkegaard developed his views in
emphatic opposition to prevailing opinions, including certain
metaphysical claims about the relation of thought to existence.
It describes his reaction to the ethical and religious theories of
Kant and Hegel, and it also contrasts his position with doctrines
currently being advanced by men like Feuerbach and Marx.
Kierkegaard's seminal diagnosis of the human condition, which
emphasizes the significance of individual choice, has arguably
been his most striking philosophical legacy, particularly for
the growth of existentialism. Both that and his arresting but
paradoxical conception of religious belief are critically discussed, Patrick Gardiner concluding this lucid introduction by
indicating salient ways in which they have impinged on contemporary thought.

PAST MASTERS

General Editor: Keith Thomas

The *Past Masters* series offers students and general readers alike concise introductions to the lives and works of the world's greatest literary figures, composers, philosophers, religious leaders, scientists, and social and political thinkers.

'Put end to end, this series will constitute a noble encyclopaedia of the history of ideas.' Mary Warnock

HOBBES

Richard Tuck

Thomas Hobbes (1588–1679) was the first great English political philosopher, and his book *Leviathan* was one of the first truly modern works of philosophy. He has long had the reputation of being a pessimistic atheist, who saw human nature as inevitably evil, and who proposed a totalitarian state to subdue human failings. In this new study, Richard Tuck shows that while Hobbes may indeed have been an atheist, he was far from pessimistic about human nature, nor did he advocate totalitarianism. By locating him against the context of his age, Dr Tuck reveals Hobbs to have been passionately concerned with the refutation of scepticism in both science and ethics, and to have developed a theory of knowledge which rivalled that of Descartes in its importance for the formation of modern philosophy.

Also available in Past Masters:

Spinoza   Roger Scruton
Bach   Denis Arnold
Machiavelli   Quentin Skinner
Darwin   Jonathan Howard

PHILOSOPHY IN OXFORD PAPERBACKS

Ranging from authoritative introductions in the Past Masters and OPUS series to in-depth studies of classical and modern thought, the Oxford Paperbacks' philosophy list is one of the most provocative and challenging available.

THE GREAT PHILOSOPHERS

Bryan Magee

Beginning with the death of Socrates in 399, and following the story through the centuries to recent figures such as Bertrand Russell and Wittgenstein, Bryan Magee and fifteen contemporary writers and philosophers provide an accessible and exciting introduction to Western philosophy and its greatest thinkers.

Bryan Magee in conversation with:

A. J. Ayer	John Passmore
Michael Ayers	Anthony Quinton
Miles Burnyeat	John Searle
Frederick Copleston	Peter Singer
Hubert Dreyfus	J. P. Stern
Anthony Kenny	Geoffrey Warnock
Sidney Morgenbesser	Bernard Williams
Martha Nussbaum	

'Magee is to be congratulated . . . anyone who sees the programmes or reads the book will be left in no danger of believing philosophical thinking is unpractical and uninteresting.' Ronald Hayman, *Times Educational Supplement*

'one of the liveliest, fast-paced introductions to philosophy, ancient and modern that one could wish for' *Universe*

Also by Bryan Magee in Oxford Paperbacks:

Men of Ideas
Aspects of Wagner 2/e

OPUS

General Editors: Christopher Butler,
Robert Evans, Alan Ryan

A HISTORY OF WESTERN PHILOSOPHY

This series of OPUS books offers a comprehensive and up-to-date survey of the history of philosophical ideas from earliest times. Its aim is not only to set those ideas in their immediate cultural context, but also to focus on their value and relevance to twentieth-century thinking.

CLASSICAL THOUGHT

Terence Irwin

Spanning over a thousand years from Homer to Saint Augustine, *Classical Thought* encompasses a vast range of material, in succinct style, while remaining clear and lucid even to those with no philosophical or Classical background.

The major philosophers and philosophical schools are examined—the Presocratics, Socrates, Plato, Aristotle, Stoicism, Epicureanism, Neoplatonism; but other important thinkers, such as Greek tragedians, historians, medical writers, and early Christian writers, are also discussed. The emphasis is naturally on questions of philosophical interest (although the literary and historical background to Classical philosophy is not ignored), and again the scope is broad—ethics, the theory of knowledge, philosophy of mind, philosophical theology. All this is presented in a fully integrated, highly readable text which covers many of the most important areas of ancient thought and in which stress is laid on the variety and continuity of philosophical thinking after Aristotle.

Also available in the History of Western Philosophy series:

The Rationalists John Cottingham
Continental Philosophy since 1750 Robert C. Solomon
The Empiricists R. S. Woolhouse

LAW FROM OXFORD PAPERBACKS

Oxford Paperbacks's law list ranges from introductions to the English legal system to reference books and in-depth studies of contemporary legal issues.

INTRODUCTION TO ENGLISH LAW
Tenth Edition

William Geldart
Edited by D. C. M. Yardley

'Geldart' has over the years established itself as a standard account of English law, expounding the body of modern law as set in its historical context. Regularly updated since its first publication, it remains indispensable to student and layman alike as a concise, reliable guide.

Since publication of the ninth edition in 1984 there have been important court decisions and a great deal of relevant new legislation. D. C. M. Yardley, Chairman of the Commission for Local Administration in England, has taken account of all these developments and the result has been a considerable rewriting of several parts of the book. These include the sections dealing with the contractual liability of minors, the abolition of the concept of illegitimacy, the liability of a trade union in tort for inducing a person to break his/her contract of employment, the new public order offences, and the intent necessary for a conviction of murder.

Other law titles:

Freedom Under Thatcher: Civil Liberties in Modern Britain
Keith Ewing and Conor Gearty
Doing the Business   Dick Hobbs
Judges   David Pannick
Law and Modern Society   P. S. Atiyah